GERMAN GRAMMAR

Norman Paxton
M.A., M.Litt., M.Ed., Ph.D.

TEACH YOURSELF BOOKS
Hodder and Stoughton

For Timothy and Angela

First published 1986
Third impression 1988

Copyright © 1986
Norman Paxton

British Library Cataloguing in Publication Data

Paxton, N.
    German grammar.—(Teach yourself books)
    1. German language—Grammar—1950–
    I. Title
    438.2′421   PF3112

ISBN 0 340 39147 2

Printed and bound in Great Britain for
Hodder and Stoughton Educational,
a division of Hodder and Stoughton Ltd,
Mill Road, Dunton Green, Sevenoaks, Kent,
by Richard Clay Ltd, Bungay, Suffolk.

Typeset by Macmillan India Ltd, Bangalore 25.

Contents

Part Three   *Putting It Together*

Introduction

Most grammar books consist purely of a statement or description of how a language operates, usually divided into unwieldy sections of varying length. They range from very concise selections of the main outlines, perhaps with titles like 'skeleton grammar', 'basis and essentials' or 'fundamentals of grammar on one card', to very fat volumes with many thousands of examples and exceptions showing even the most subtle distinctions. They are not intended to be read right through, but rather as works of reference. This *Teach Yourself German Grammar*, on the other hand, is designed to facilitate learning. To this end the grammar is not merely presented but explained, and chapters indicating what the grammatical forms are alternate with chapters showing how these forms are used. Moreover the chapters have been kept short, as digestible as possible, and of fairly even length.

If knowledge of a language may be taken as comprising an understanding of the words it uses, together with an understanding of how they are combined to form meaningful utterances, then the former is what is commonly termed vocabulary (known to professional linguists as lexis), and the latter is what is called grammar. It is obvious that the grammar can be demonstrated only by using words occurring in the lexis (or dictionary) of the language. If these words are chosen at random, they will include some which rarely occur in everyday use. This may constitute an additional and possibly unnecessary difficulty for the student, since it may fairly be assumed that anyone finding it advisable to read a German grammar is unlikely to be familiar with the rarer words of the language. Most German grammars, however, do not appear to have taken this fact into account. In this book, the words used in examples have been selected from the list of the 3000 words occurring most frequently in contemporary German, as established by I. Kosaras in *Grundwortschatz der deutschen Sprache* (Berlin 1980), with just a few additions: it was felt, for example, that the omission from the list of **Engländerin** (*Englishwoman*) should be remedied. This is not to say that all 3000 words will appear in this book – far from it! (we use in fact less than half that number) – but that the reader may be assured that all the words which do appear are common, of very frequent occurrence, and therefore well worth learning.

Just as no-one attempts to learn the whole dictionary of a language, so no-one feels it necessary to memorise every detail of the largest German grammar, with its multitude of inexplicable and often esoteric exceptions. This book attempts to confine itself to the grammar it is really necessary to know if one is to understand, and be able to express oneself in, everyday German. Some people say they do not bother about grammar at all, and are sure they get all the tenses and endings wrong, yet they seem to 'get by'. If you ever actually get the opportunity to observe such individuals in action, you will almost certainly feel that you would like to progress beyond this 'Me Tarzan You Jane' level of language use. Many shrink from tackling grammar because their undoubted knowledge of the grammar of their native language is unconscious, and the condensed and formulated way in which grammar is summarised in a grammar book seems to them impossible to assimilate. This fear is quite groundless: grammar is simply the way in which words should be arranged to give the best chance of successful communication, and if you learn a language through its grammar instead of through a phrase book, then each phrase will be seen as representative of countless other utterances of similar pattern, and not just one utterance set in aspic, as it were.

A rewarding side-effect of any consideration of German grammar is the light it sheds on English grammar: both languages (together with Dutch and the Scandinavian languages) belong to the Germanic family of languages, and they have more in common, especially grammatically, than, say, English and French or English and Welsh, where other language families (Romance and Celtic respectively) are involved. Such concepts as strong verbs and inseparable prefixes suddenly become less terrifying when one realises that we have them in English too. Many English learners profess surprise on learning that there are rules in German about the order of words in a sentence: they fondly imagine that English has none, and yet they would be nonplussed if a certain old Beatles song came out as *Me money love buy can't* or indeed in any other unfamiliar order. Reading an outline of German grammar sets one thinking on such matters, and deepens one's awareness of how the English language operates.

The reader is recommended initially to go straight through this book fairly quickly, to become aware of its modest dimensions and steady pace. It does not matter if some chapters are not immediately clear on first reading: they can be returned to and digested as slowly as need be. The book has been constructed to meet the needs of a variety of readers. It may be a refresher course for those wanting to brush up a rusty knowledge of German gained years ago at school. It can enable those whose interest stems from holidays in Austria, Germany or Switzerland to exchange the crutch of a phrase book for the springboard of infinitely wider applications that a knowledge of grammar provides. Those with no previous knowledge of German, and who perhaps require a reading knowledge only, will find that, since every example is translated into English and the vocabulary is limited, this book places their goal within their grasp. Those attending conversation classes, which almost by definition must devote very little time to grammar, will find it an invaluable adjunct.

There is a widespread mistrust of grammar on the part of learners who feel that the 'right' way to learn a language must be 'nature's way', i.e. the way one learns one's mother tongue, but this is to ignore the fact that such a procedure would be utterly impossible. A baby acquires language over a period of many years, during which it is hearing the language around it in all its waking hours. It begins with a lengthy period of listening only (which few adults could tolerate) and then proceeds purely by imitation and analogy, in which it has the undivided attention and monitoring of its parents. These circumstances could not be reproduced for the adult learner, even if he or she could afford the time span involved. Much better to capitalise on the advantage one has as an adult of being capable of comprehending the idea of language as a system and thereby learn more efficiently by noting the rules imparted by a grammatical approach – indeed many students in adult education classes taught by 'direct' or 'no grammar' methods feel keenly a need to acquire some grasp of the grammar.

The study of grammar seems at first sight difficult to many readers because, like every other systematic presentation of knowledge, it employs a number of technical terms and needs its own jargon to express itself concisely. The number of indispensable grammatical terms is between fifty and a hundred, and an adequate definition of each one would require more space than is available here, so a few will be taken for granted, namely those which are very basic concepts in English (e.g. noun, verb, sentence). All those which are not commonly used in English will be explained (e.g. case, gender, subjunctive). In fact, all these terms are useful time-saving abbreviations, and occurring, as they do in this book, beside simple examples illustrating them, they need not intimidate anyone.

German, more than most languages, startles the learner by the apparent complexity of its spelling and the seemingly inordinate length of some of its compound words. In fact German is easier to pronounce correctly than, say, English or French, by virtue of the fact that it is consistently pronounced exactly as it is spelt. Once one has got over the shock of realising that a word spelt **Pfropf** is indeed pronounced **p-f-r-o-p-f** and that **tsch** is simply English *ch*, there are few difficulties of pronunciation. Such as there are are explained in detail in Appendix I 'The Sounds of German', which offers a complete guide to pronunciation, stress and syllabification. The long compound words lose their terrors as soon as one realises that, firstly, German likes to present what is clearly one idea as one word, whereas English is accustomed to indicate subsidiary components of that idea by separate words (thus a *Life Assurance Company*, which is clearly one entity, is in German a **Lebensversicherungsgesellschaft**, written as one word), and secondly, the elements which make up these compound words are usually more self-explanatory in German than in English (thus a woman having her first baby is in English medically termed *primiparous*, but in German **erstmalgebärig** i.e. first-time-childbearing). The way such compound words are built up, and how they may be broken down for comprehension, is clearly set out in Appendix II 'The Structure of the German Vocabulary', together with other clues by which the meaning of an unknown German word may be deduced.

Appendix III provides, as is incumbent on any grammar book, a list of strong and irregular verbs. Whereas, however, most grammar books give a long (and hence very indigestible) list alphabetically, this book gives only those verbs common in everyday use, and groups them to indicate that 'I sing, I sang, I have sung' belongs with 'I drink, I drank, I have drunk', whereas 'I bring, I brought, I have brought' belongs with 'I think, I thought, I have thought' (even though it has been argued that the learner who postulates 'I bring, I brang, I have brung' has really got the hang of what is a strong verb!). It is hoped that this will greatly facilitate the learning of this essential but tedious task.

For the most part, though, the learning of German grammar need not be tedious. On the contrary, an *understanding* of the rules and structure of German brings its own satisfaction, as well as insights which will be of practical value in studying and using the language. If this book, with its emphasis on explanation and modern usage, contributes to that understanding, it will have achieved all it set out to do.

PART ONE
The Noun and Its Associates

1 Some Basic Terms

Certain grammatical features which are important in the basic structure of the German language are unfamiliar to the English speaker and need to be understood from the outset. Among the most important are the concepts termed case, declension, gender and agreement.

Articles, adjectives and nouns vary their form in German to convey extra information both about their function in the sentence and their relationship to other words in it. These forms are called **cases**, and there are four which occur in German (Finnish has fourteen!). When a noun is the subject of a sentence, the **nominative** case is used. Thus in Der Mann ist groß* *The man is tall*, **Der Mann** is in the nominative case. When a noun is the direct object of a sentence, the **accusative** case is used. Thus in Ich kenne den Mann *I know the man*, **den Mann** is in the accusative case. When possession or dependence is indicated, the **genitive** case is used. Thus in Der Sohn des Mannes spielt *The man's son* [*the son of the man*] *is playing*, **des Mannes** is in the genitive case (but **der Sohn** is in the nominative because he is the subject). When a noun is the indirect object or recipient in a sentence, the **dative** case is used. Thus in Ich gebe dem Mann den Scheck *I give* [*to*] *the man the cheque*, **dem Mann** is in the dative case (but **den Scheck** is in the accusative, because it is the direct object).

In addition to these functions it will be necessary to note that prepositions are followed by particular cases and that certain verbs are followed by the dative or genitive case, but these will be dealt with later in the book. Note also that nouns in German always begin with a capital letter – this makes them very easy to identify.

---

* Note the letter ß, called **eszett** or **scharfes s**, which is to all intents and purposes a double *s*, but is generally used instead of *ss*, which is retained only between vowels if the first of these is short (all diphthongs count as long). Thus **der Fluß** (*the river*) has the plural **die Flüsse**, but **der Fuß** (*the foot*) has the plural **die Füße**. The rules enabling one to determine which vowels are short and which are long are set out in Appendix I. Cf. also **wir lassen** (*we leave*) but **ihr laßt** (*you leave*), **reißen** (*to tear*) but **gerissen** (*torn*). A few proper names are exceptions: Günter Grass, Carl Zeiss.

The table of a noun's nominative, accusative, genitive and dative forms in the singular and plural is known as the declension of that noun. The plural of **Mann** is **Männer**, thus the full declension of **der Mann** is:

MASCULINE	*Singular*	*Plural*
Nominative	der Mann	die Männer
Accusative	den Mann	die Männer
Genitive	des Mann(e)s	der Männer
Dative	dem Mann	den Männern

The observant reader will have noticed that not all the cases of the noun differ in form: there are only four different forms, i.e. **Mann**, **Mann(e)s**, **Männer** and **Männern**, among the eight cases of the full declension. The bracket in **Mann(e)s** indicates that **Manns** and **Mannes** are both acceptable – the **e** is optional. The definite article (the word for *the*) distinguishes more fully – only the nominative plural and accusative plural are identical.

The statement that **Mann** (*man*) is a masculine noun is equally meaningful and true in English and German. Whereas in English, however, the classification of nouns into masculine, feminine and neuter is purely biological – masculine for male beings, feminine for female beings and neuter for inanimate notions – in German these are grammatical categories without necessarily reflecting the meaning, e.g. the word **Kind** (*child*) is neuter. The term used for these categories is **gender**. There are then three genders in German, **masculine** gender, **feminine** gender and **neuter** gender, and every noun in the language belongs to one of the three. They are distinguished by having different words for the definite article. **Der** is the nominative singular form of the definite article only with *masculine* nouns. With *feminine* nouns it is **die**, and with *neuter* nouns it is **das**. As one might suspect, these have their own forms for the various cases, and the full declension of a feminine noun and of a neuter noun are as follows:

FEMININE	**die Frau** (*woman*)	*Singular*	*Plural*
Nominative		**die** Frau	**die** Frauen
Accusative		**die** Frau	**die** Frauen
Genitive		**der** Frau	**der** Frauen
Dative		**der** Frau	**den** Frauen

NEUTER	**das Kind** (*child*)	*Singular*	*Plural*
Nominative		**das** Kind	**die** Kinder
Accusative		**das** Kind	**die** Kinder
Genitive		**des** Kind(e)s	**der** Kinder
Dative		**dem** Kind	**den** Kindern

It can be seen from the three declensions given that the definite article varies according to the gender of the noun only in the singular forms: in the plural it is the same for all three genders. The full declension of the definite article is, therefore:

	Singular			**Plural**
	Masc.	*Fem.*	*Neut.*	*All genders*
Nominative	der	die	das	die
Accusative	den	die	das	die
Genitive	des	der	des	der
Dative	dem	der	dem	den

It is evident from the foregoing that if a masculine singular noun is in the genitive, then the definite article before it must be in the masculine singular genitive form too (as in **Der Sohn des Mannes spielt**). The technical term for this is **agreement**, and the article is said to **agree** with the noun in gender, number (i.e. singular or plural) and case. It will be seen later that adjectives in front of nouns also have to agree in the same way.

Another type of agreement is that between a verb and its subject. These must agree in 'person', as when in English if the subject is *he*, then the verb *walk* must have an *s*: *he walks*. The person speaking (usually *I* or *we*) is termed the first person, the person spoken to (*you* or perhaps *thou*) is the second person, and the person or thing spoken about (which might be *he, she, it, they* or *the ghost of Jacob Marley*) is the third person, whether it is a person or not. All three may obviously be either singular or plural, so that there are six persons altogether.

The term definite article (meaning the word for *the*) is complemented by the term indefinite article, which refers to the word for *a* or *an*. This declines as shown overleaf:

	Masc.	*Fem.*	*Neut.*
Nominative	ein	eine	ein
Accusative	einen	eine	ein
Genitive	eines	einer	eines
Dative	einem	einer	einem

Notice that the diphthong **ei** (as in **ein**) is pronounced like English *ei* in *height*, whereas **ie** (as in **die**) is pronounced like English *ie* in *thief*; be careful not to confuse them.

The indefinite article has of course no plural, the plural of **ein Mann** being simply **Männer**. The declension of the indefinite article closely resembles that of the singular definite article: both could be represented as:

--	**-e**	--
-en	**-e**	--
-es	**-er**	**-es**
-em	**-er**	**-em**

The definite article provides a pattern for the declension of a number of common adjectives, the most important of which are **dieser** (*this*), **jeder** (*each* or *every*), **jener** (*that* – cf. English *yon*), **mancher** (*many, many a*), **solcher** (*such, such a*) and **welcher** (*which*). In other words these decline identically, for example:

	Singular			**Plural**
	Masc.	*Fem.*	*Neut.*	*All genders*
Nominative	dieser	diese	dieses	diese
Accusative	diesen	diese	dieses	diese
Genitive	dieses	dieser	dieses	dieser
Dative	diesem	dieser	diesem	diesen

Similarly the indefinite article provides a pattern for the declension of all the possessive adjectives and of the word **kein** (*no, not a*) with the addition of the plural endings of the definite article. The possessive adjectives are: **mein** (*my*), **sein** (*his, its*), **ihr** (*her, its, their*), **unser** (*our*), **Ihr** (*your*), plus two so-called familiar forms (corresponding to the obsolete English forms *thou* and *ye*), the second person singular **dein** (*your, thy*) and plural **euer** (*your*). These two are unlikely to be needed by the English learner except for recognition purposes, as their chief use is between members of the same family and very close friends. The only peculiarity of declension among the possessive adjectives is that those which are not monosyllables (**unser** and **euer**) tend to drop an 'e' rather than become three syllables long, so that one gets **unsern** or **unsren** and not **unseren**, and **eures**, **eurem**, not **eueres**, **euerem**. The typical declension of a possessive adjective, then, is as follows:

	Singular			**Plural**
	Masc.	*Fem.*	*Neut.*	*All genders*
Nominative	mein	meine	mein	meine
Accusative	meinen	meine	mein	meine
Genitive	meines	meiner	meines	meiner
Dative	meinem	meiner	meinem	meinen

Note that the **dieser** and **mein** declensions differ only in the nominative masculine singular and the nominative and accusative neuter singular: the remaining thirteen endings are common to both declensions.

In addition to explaining the terms *case, declension, gender* and *agreement*, this chapter has shown how the definite and indefinite articles are declined in full, and demonstrated those words which decline like them. The next chapter will show how these articles and related words are used, and in particular how their use in German differs from their use in English.

2 The Use of Articles and Related Words

If one were to list all the instances in which an article must be used in German, and point out all the cases where no article is used, the list would number many hundreds of items. Fortunately, however, the overwhelming majority would coincide with English usage, because German and English are members of the same Germanic family of languages. For example, a sentence like *Gold and silver are metals* (**Gold und Silber sind Metalle**) would have no articles in either German or English, whereas it would require articles in French. In general, then, articles are used in German much as in English, and we may confine our attention to those cases where they are not.

The definite article is used in German:

(a) before many abstract nouns and nouns (usually plural) used in a generalised sense:
das Alter *old age* das Leben *life* die Ehe *marriage* die Freiheit *freedom* die Jugend *youth* die Arbeit *work* der Schlaf *sleep* die Wahrheit *truth*.
Die Preise sind stabil. *Prices are steady*.
Die Zeiten ändern sich. *Times change*.

(b) before proper nouns if they are preceded by an adjective:
der alte Heinz *old Heinz* **das** schöne Deutschland *beautiful Germany*

(c) in expressions of price or quantity (where English would use *a* or *per*):
Es kostet acht Mark **das** Kilo. *It costs eight marks a kilo*.
Er fuhr neunzig Kilometer **die** Stunde. *He drove at ninety kilometres an hour*.

(d) with names of countries unless they are neuter singular (which most of them are):
Er wohnt **in** England. *He lives in England*.

BUT

Er wohnt **in der** Tschechoslowakei. *He lives in Czechoslovakia.*
Er fährt **nach** Frankreich. *He is travelling to France.*

BUT

Er fährt **nach der** Schweiz. *He is travelling to Switzerland.*

Der Libanon liegt südlich **von der** Türkei. aber sehr weit **von** Australien. *Lebanon lies south of Turkey, but a long way from Australia.*

(*e*) with reference to items of clothing or parts of the body, where English would use a possessive adjective:

Er hat sich **das** Bein verletzt. *He hurt his leg.*
Sie zog **den** Mantel aus. *She took her coat off.*

(*f*) with days, months, seasons and meals:

Der Mittwoch ist frei. *Wednesday is free.*
Der Juni ist immer warm. *June is always warm.*
Der Winter ist immer kalt. *Winter is always cold.*
nach **dem** Frühstück *after breakfast*

(*g*) with the names of streets or squares, but not when giving addresses:

Der Kennedyplatz ist gerade in der Stadtmitte. *Kennedy Square is right in the town centre.*

Der Bahnhof liegt in **der** Königsstraße. *The station is in King Street.*

BUT

Ich wohne Hauptstraße 48. *I live at 48 Main Street.*

(*h*) to indicate that a noun is in the genitive or dative case:

ein Ausdruck **des** Erstaunens *an expression of astonishment*
Ich ziehe Tee **dem** Kaffee vor. *I prefer tea to coffee.*

(*i*) with the adjective **meist** (*most*):

In **den meisten** Fällen muß man zwei Wochen warten. *In most cases one has to wait two weeks.*

Das meiste davon habe ich vergessen. *I have forgotten most of it.*
Die meisten Leute glauben das nicht. *Most people don't believe that.*

(*j*) in many set phrases frequently encountered, of which the following are only a sample:

mit dem Zug (Schiff etc.) *by train (boat etc.)* mit der Post *by post*
Dem Himmel sei Dank! *Thank Heavens!* in der Kirche *in church*
in der Stadt *in town* in der Schule *in school*
Sie ist die Güte selbst. *She is kindness itself.* in der Tat *in fact*

The definite article is omitted in German, where it would be used in English:

(*a*) in legal, military and other jargon or officialese:

Es ist nicht Sache dieses Gerichtes. *It is not the business of this court.*

Auf Befehl des Kommandanten. *On the orders of the commander.*

Ich, Unterzeichneter, erkläre hiermit, daß . . . *I, the undersigned, hereby declare that . . .*

(*b*) often before an adjective preceding a noun:

Jüngstes Mitglied der Mannschaft ist Schmidt. *The youngest member of the team is Smith.*

Nehmen wir folgendes Beispiel: *Let us take the following example*:

bei bestem Willen *with the best will in the world*

(*c*) in many set phrases frequently encountered, of which the following are only a sample:

Sie hören Nachrichten. *You are listening to the news.* (*Here is the news.*)

Es ist Mode geworden. *It has become the fashion.*

nach Kriegsende *after the end of the war*

Hauptsache ist . . . *The main thing is . . .*

Das ist bei uns so Sitte. *That is the custom with us.*

The use of the indefinite article in German corresponds even more closely with English, but the following instances should be noted where English uses an indefinite article and German does not:

(*a*) after **sein, werden** and **bleiben** (provided there is no adjective), when indicating profession, nationality or religion:

Er ist Lehrer. *He is a teacher.*

Mein Mann ist Katholik. *My husband is a Catholic.*

Er wurde Oberst. *He became a Colonel.*

Er blieb Soldat. *He remained a soldier.*

Mein Mann ist Deutscher. *My husband is a German.*

BUT

Er ist **ein** guter Lehrer. *He is a good teacher.*

(*b*) after **als** meaning *as a*:

Ich spreche **als** Engländer. *I speak as an Englishman.*

Das gab er mir **als** Geschenk. *He gave me that as a present.*

(*c*) the so-called 'adverbial genitive', for example:

Er verabschiedete sich leichten Herzens. *He took his leave with a light heart.*

Sie ist guter Laune. *She is in a good mood.*

(*d*)   a number of idiomatic expressions, such as:
   Das ist Geschmacksache. *That is a matter of taste.*
   Freitags ist Sitzung. *There is a meeting on Fridays.*
   Es ist Tatsache, daß . . . *It is a fact that . . .*
   Ich habe Kopfschmerzen. *I have a headache.*

The use of **dieser, jeder, jener, mancher, solcher** and **welcher**, which decline like the definite article, presents few problems. It is worth noting that, firstly, **dieser** is very often used where English would have *that* and not *this*:

   Er arbeitete fleißig in **diesen** Jahren.   *He worked hard in those days.*
   Diese Route würde ich nicht empfehlen.   *I wouldn't recommend that route.*

Secondly, **jener** is used chiefly in contrast with **dieser** or to indicate remoteness:

   Diese Geschichte ist noch langweiliger als **jene**.   *This story is even more boring than that one.*
   Ich erinnere mich **jenes** Tages noch genau.   *I can still vividly remember that day.*

Thirdly, **jener** and **dieser** are also used to mean *the former* and *the latter* respectively:

   Jean und Paco sind Ausländer: **dieser** ist Spanier, **jener** Franzose.   *Jean and Paco are foreigners: the latter is Spanish, the former French.*

In this usage **dieser**, i.e. *this one*, is used to refer to the second noun, which is the closer one, and **jener** refers to the first noun, which is the more distant. This is really quite logical.

Solcher on its own is declined like **dieser**, but before **ein** it is undeclined:

   Ich habe nie **solchen** Hunger gehabt.   *I have never been so hungry.*
   Solch einen Wein habe ich nie getrunken. OR **Einen solchen** Wein habe ich nie getrunken.   *I have never drunk a wine like this.*

The same applies to **mancher**: Das ist schon **manchem** passiert. *That has happened to many a man.* The uninflected form **manch**, however, is archaic and rarely found: manch gute Frau *many a good woman.*

Among the words which decline like **mein**, special attention should be paid to **kein** (*not a, not any, no*), variously called a negative article, negative adjective or indefinite adjective, which is often used where one would expect **nicht ein**:

Wir haben **kein** Auto. *We haven't a car.*

Ich habe **keinen** Teller. *I haven't got a plate.*

Er hat **keine** Zeit. *He has no time.*

Sie ist **kein** Kind mehr. *She's no longer a child.*

Ich möchte lieber **kein** Bier. *I'd rather not have any beer.*

Er sagte **kein** Wort. *He didn't say a word.*

Nicht ein (*not one*) may be used if it is desired to stress the *one*:

Nicht ein Soldat wurde verletzt. *Not one soldier was wounded.*

The use of possessive adjectives is basically as in English, but note that they have to be repeated before each noun even when these are of the same gender:

mein Bruder und **meine** Schwester *my brother and sister*

Gib mir **meinen** Hut und **meinen** Mantel! *Give me my hat and coat!*

This chapter has listed and given examples of instances where the use of the articles and related words is different in German and English. The definite article and its related words (**dieser**, **jeder**, **jener**, **mancher**, **solcher**, **welcher**) will be referred to in this book as 'der words', and words which decline like **kein** (possessive adjectives and **ein** in the singular) will be referred to as '**mein** words'. The next chapter will deal with the gender of nouns.

3 The Gender of Nouns

Note first of all that all nouns in German are written with a capital letter.

One of the chief difficulties in learning German nouns is remembering the gender of each noun, and it cannot be too strongly emphasised that a German noun should always be memorised together with its definite article: learn the German for *school* not as **Schule** but as **die Schule**, and *house* not as **Haus** but as **das Haus**.

This chapter offers some help towards identifying groups of nouns belonging to each gender, distinguishing between those which have that gender by form, e.g. by having a certain prefix or suffix, and those which have that gender by meaning, e.g. the names of most countries are neuter (as mentioned in the previous chapter), whereas seasons, months and days of the week are masculine.

Masculine by form

These include the following:

1 Nouns ending in **-ich, -ig, -ing, -ling**:

der Stich	*sting*	der Strich	*line*
der Käfig	*cage*	der König	*king*
der Ring	*ring*	der Hering	*herring*
der Zwilling	*twin*	der Lehrling	*apprentice*

Exceptions: das Ding *thing*, das Camping *camping*.

2 Nouns of foreign origin ending in **-an, -ast, -ent** (except for most words ending in **-ment**), **-ismus, -ist, -or**:

der Ozean	*ocean*	der Roman	*novel*
der Palast	*palace*	der Plast	*plastic*
der Akzent	*accent*	der Präsident	*president*
der Sozialismus	*socialism*	der Kommunismus	*communism*
der Komponist	*composer*	der Polizist	*policeman*
der Professor	*professor*	der Motor	*motor*

Exceptions: das Organ *organ* das Prozent *percent*,
das Talent *talent* das Tor *gate, goal*.

Masculine by meaning

These include the following:

1 Days, months, seasons and points of the compass:
   der Mittwoch　*Wednesday*　　der Donnerstag　*Thursday*
   der März　*March*　　　　　　der Dezember　*December*
   der Frühling　*spring*　　　　der Herbst　*autumn*
   der Süden　*south*　　　　　　der Nordosten　*north-east*

2 Weather features:
   der Regen　*rain*　　der Schnee　*snow*　der Frost　*frost*
   der Nebel　*fog*　　　der Wind　*wind* – and the names of all
   　　　　　　　　　　winds

3 Makes of motor cars (**der Wagen** (*car*) being understood):
   der Ford, der Mercedes, der Fiat, der Opel, der BMW, der
   Renault

4 Male persons and animals:
   der Mann　*man*　der Bruder　*brother*　der Sohn　*son*
   der Arzt　*doctor*　der Bäcker　*baker*　der Tischler　*joiner*
   der Fuchs　*fox*　der Hund　*dog*　　der Löwe　*lion*

Feminine by form

These include the following:

1 Nouns formed from masculine nouns by adding **-in** to give the
   female equivalent:
   die Ärztin　*woman doctor*　　die Löwin　*lioness*
   die Freundin　*female friend*　die Engländerin
   　　　　　　　　　　　　　　　Englishwoman

2 Nouns ending in **-ei**, **-heit**, **-keit**, **-schaft**, **-ung**:
   die Arznei　*medicament*　　die Druckerei　*printing works*
   die Gesundheit　*health*　　die Einzelheit　*detail*
   die Aufmerksamkeit　*attention*　die Geschwindigkeit　*speed*
   die Gemeinschaft　*community*　die Erklärung　*explanation*
   die Forschung　*research*　　die Gesellschaft　*company,*
   　　　　　　　　　　　　　　　society

3 Nouns of foreign origin ending in **-a**, **-anz**, **-enz**, **-ie**, **-ik**, **-ion**, **-tät**,
   -ur:
   die Prosa　*prose*　　　　　die Firma　*firm*
   die Toleranz　*tolerance*　　die Eleganz　*elegance*
   die Konferenz　*conference*　die Intelligenz　*intelligence*

die Melodie	*melody*	die Industrie	*industry*
die Kritik	*criticism*	die Republik	*republic*
die Illusion	*illusion*	die Infektion	*infection*
die Elektrizität	*electricity*	die Qualität	*quality*
die Temperatur	*temperature*	die Figur	*figure*

Exceptions: das Sofa   *sofa*,   das Genie   *genius*,
das Stadion   *stadium*

Feminine by meaning

These include the following:

1   Most trees and flowers:

die Buche	*beech*	die Eiche	*oak*	die Lärche	*larch*
die Nelke	*carnation*	die Rose	*rose*	die Tulpe	*tulip*

2   Nouns formed from adjectives of dimension:

die Breite *width* from **breit** *wide*	die Dichte *density* from **dicht** *dense*
die Dicke *thickness* from **dick** *thick*	die Ferne *distance* from **fern** *far*
die Größe *size* from **groß** *big*	die Höhe *height* from **hoch** *high*
die Länge *length* from **lang** *long*	die Schwere *weight* from **schwer** *heavy*

3   Female persons and animals:

die Frau	*lady*	die Tante	*aunt*	die Tochter	*daughter*
die Katze	*cat*	die Kuh	*cow*	die Sau	*sow*

Exception: das Weib *woman, wife* – old-fashioned or pejorative.
See also Neuter nouns 1. below (**das Fräulein, das Mädchen**)

Neuter by form

These include the following:

1   Nouns ending in **-lein, -chen, -nis, -tel, -tum**:

das Fräulein	*young lady*	das Männlein	*little man*
das Mädchen	*girl*	das Häuschen	*little house*
das Hindernis	*hindrance*	das Ergebnis	*result*
das Drittel	*third*	das Viertel	*quarter*
das Christentum	*Christianity*	das Eigentum	*property*

Exceptions: die Erlaubnis   *permission*,
die Kenntnis   *knowledge*,
der Irrtum   *error*, der Reichtum   *wealth*.

2   Collective nouns beginning with the prefix **Ge-**:
das Geschirr *crockery*   das Geräusch *noise*   das Gebäck
cakes & biscuits

das Gemüse *vegetables*   das Gepäck *luggage*
das Geschrei   *shouting*
Exceptions: der Geruch *smell*, der Gesang *song*,
die Gemeinde *congregation*.

3   Nouns of foreign origin ending in **-at, -ma, -ment, -um, -ium**:
das Quadrat   *square*   das Zitat   *quotation*
das Komma   *comma*   das Thema   *topic*
das Dokument   *document*   das Experiment   *experiment*
das Album   *album*   das Datum   *date*
das Studium *study*   das Laboratorium   *laboratory*
Exceptions: der Salat *salad*, der Zement *cement*.

Neuter by meaning

These include the following:

1   Chemical elements:
das Eisen   *iron*   das Chlor   *chlorine*   das Gold   *gold*
das Jod   *iodine*   das Kupfer   *copper*   das Silber   *silver*
Exceptions: der Phosphor *phosphorus*, der Schwefel *sulphur*.

2   Other parts of speech, also letters of the alphabet, when used as
nouns:
Das **Schwimmen** ist sehr gesund. *Swimming is very healthy.*

VERB

Das **Wichtige** siehst du nicht! *You can't see the important thing!*

ADJECTIVE

Man muß das **Für** und **Wider** erwägen. *One must weigh the pros
and cons.*   PREPOSITION

Er sagt das endgültige **Nein**. *He says the final no.*   ADVERB

Das **Ob** und **Wie** besprechen wir später. *We'll discuss later
whether and how to proceed.*   CONJUNCTION

Er hat mir das **Du** angeboten. *He suggested we call each other 'Du'.*

PRONOUN

Bei Callas war das hohe **C** unvergeßlich. *Callas' top C was
unforgettable.*   ALPHABET

3   Most countries and continents, and all towns except **den Haag**:
das alte Wien   *old Vienna*   das heutige Europa
Europe today

das schöne Norwegen   das neue Afrika *new Africa*
    beautiful Norway

Exceptions: countries with names ending in -e, -ei, -z are feminine:
die Türkei *Turkey*, die Tschechoslowakei *Czechoslovakia*, die Schweiz *Switzerland*, die Pfalz *Palatinate*, die Ukraine *Ukraine*, die Simbabwe *Zimbabwe*.

Here, then, are eighteen categories, six for each gender, where the gender may be recalled or known by the form or function of the word itself. They are not the only possible ones, but the ones judged to be of most practical use. Other grammars will tell you that, for example, most nouns ending in -e are feminine, or most -er nouns masculine. That is true, but the number of exceptions even in any basic German vocabulary is so large as to make the rule hardly worth learning. The exceptions given above are not necessarily the only ones in the German language, but they are the only ones occurring among the very commonest words in German. Some of the rules are not so arbitrary as they may seem: the reason why *young lady* and *girl* are neuter is that the suffixes -lein and -chen indicate diminutive forms (*little lady, little maid*) and are always neuter. There are many words with the prefix Ge- which are not neuter, but they are not truly collective nouns. As you become more and more familiar with more and more words, you will find that you acquire and build up a certain 'feeling for the language' (das Sprachgefühl), and the problem of gender will cease to be a bewilderment. Notice, incidentally, how neatly German expresses in the three-syllable word Sprachgefühl, a concept which needs six syllables and four words in English! Meanwhile, this chapter may be referred back to as often as necessary – it can hardly be digested at one swallow.

We saw in Chapter 1 that nouns (e.g. Mann, Frau, Kind) do not all decline in exactly the same way. The next chapter sets out the main declensions and indicates groups of nouns which decline similarly.

4 The Declension of Nouns

There are almost as many ways of classifying German noun declensions as there are grammar books, and the number of types differentiated varies from five to well over twenty, but the essential distinction, which is still valid, was first made by the German philologist Jakob Grimm (1785–1863), better known for his collaboration with his brother Wilhelm in publishing *Grimm's Fairy Tales* (***Kinder- und Hausmärchen***) in 1812–14. He divided nouns into what he termed weak, strong and mixed declensions.

Weak declensions

The weak declension comprises all nouns which add **-n** or **-en** to the nominative singular to form all the other cases both singular and plural, without making any other change, as with **der Student** (*student*) below:

	Singular		*Plural*	
Nom.	der	Student	die	Studenten
Acc.	den	Studenten	die	Studenten
Gen.	des	Studenten	der	Studenten
Dat.	dem	Studenten	den	Studenten

Common nouns which belong to this declension include **der Bayer** (*Bavarian*), **der Christ** (*Christian*), **der Held** (*hero*), **der Junge** (*boy*), **der Kamerad** (*comrade*), **der Matrose** (*sailor*), **der Mensch** (*human being*), **der Neffe** (*nephew*), **der Nerv** (*nerve*) and **der Präsident** (*president*).

The weak declension may also be considered as including almost all feminine nouns, with the proviso that all feminine nouns remain unchanged in all the singular cases (cf. *die Frau*, given in full in Chapter 1); most, however, add **-n** or **-en** to form the plural, and so markedly resemble the weak declension, as with **die Blume** (*flower*) opposite:

	Singular		Plural	
Nom.	die	Blume	die	Blumen
Acc.	die	Blume	die	Blumen
Gen.	der	Blume	der	Blumen
Dat.	der	Blume	den	Blumen

Finally, it is worth noting that there are no neuter nouns in the weak declension.

Strong declensions

The strong declensions are characterised by forming their genitive singular by adding -(e)s (except, of course, for feminine nouns). Many of them form their plural by adding an **Umlaut** (i.e. two dots over the main vowel), whether or not they add anything else. The technical term for this is 'modifying the vowel', and although we do not use the two-dot accent for this in English, we have the same phenomenon in *man/men, mouse/mice, goose/geese*. There are, however, a variety of ways of forming the plural, which may accordingly be regarded as different declensions. Some nouns, chiefly those ending in -el, -en, -er, either make no change to form the plural, as with **der Onkel** (*uncle*), or simply modify the vowel, as with **der Vater** (*father*):

	Singular		Plural		Singular		Plural	
Nom.	der	Onkel	die	Onkel	der	Vater	die	Väter
Acc.	den	Onkel	die	Onkel	den	Vater	die	Väter
Gen.	des	Onkels	der	Onkel	des	Vaters	der	Väter
Dat.	dem	Onkel	den	Onkeln	dem	Vater	den	Vätern

Common nouns which belong to this declension include those:

(a) without vowel modification: der Deckel (*lid*), das Fenster (*window*), das Gebäude (*building*), das Gemüse (*vegetable*), der Kuchen (*cake*), das Mädchen (*girl*), der Maler (*painter*), das Männlein (*little man*), der Spaten (*spade*) and der Wagen (*car*);

(b) with vowel modification: der Apfel (*apple*), der Bruder (*brother*), der Garten (*garden*), das Kloster (*monastery, convent*), der Laden (*shop*), der Mantel (*coat*), die Mutter (*mother*), der Ofen (*stove*), die Tochter (*daughter*) and der Vogel (*bird*).

Other nouns add -e to form the plural, either without vowel modification, as with **der Tag** (*day*), or with vowel modification as with **der Sohn** (*son*):

	Singular	Plural	Singular	Plural
Nom.	der Tag	die Tage	der Sohn	die Söhne
Acc.	den Tag	die Tage	den Sohn	die Söhne
Gen.	des Tag(e)s	der Tage	des Sohn(e)s	der Söhne
Dat.	dem Tag	den Tagen	dem Sohn	den Söhnen

Common nouns which belong to this declension include those:

(a)   without vowel modification: der Tisch (*table*), der Arm (*arm*), das Bein (*leg*), der Blick (*look*), der Film (*film*), das Haar (*hair*), der Hund (*dog*), das Jahr (*year*), der Laut (*sound*) and der Schuh (*shoe*);

(b)   with vowel modification: die Angst (*fear*), der Arzt (*doctor*), die Frucht (*fruit*), die Hand (*hand*), die Kuh (*cow*), die Macht (*power*), die Nacht (*night*), der Plan (*plan*), die Stadt (*town*) and die Wand (*wall*).

Note that all the words in this declension are monosyllables.

Another group of nouns forms the plural by adding -**er**, either without vowel modification as with **das Bild** (*picture*), or with vowel modification, as with **der Wald** (*forest*):

	Singular	Plural	Singular	Plural
Nom.	das Bild	die Bilder	der Wald	die Wälder
Acc.	das Bild	die Bilder	den Wald	die Wälder
Gen.	des Bild(e)s	der Bilder	des Wald(e)s	der Wälder
Dat.	dem Bild	den Bildern	dem Wald	den Wäldern

Common nouns which belong to this declension include those:

(a)   without vowel modification: das Brett (*plank*), das Ei (*egg*), das Feld (*field*), der Geist (*spirit*), das Geschlecht (*sex*), das Gesicht (*face*), das Kind (*child*), das Kleid (*dress*), das Licht (*light*) and das Lied (*song*);

(b)   with vowel modification: das Bad (*bath*), das Buch (*book*), das Dach (*roof*), das Dorf (*village*), das Eigentum (*property*), das Glas (*glass*), das Haus (*house*), der Irrtum (*error*), das Land (country) and der Mann (*man, husband*)

Finally, two oddments: feminine nouns with the suffix -**in** add -**nen** to form the plural, as with **die Löwin** (*lioness*), and some foreign nouns form their plural by adding -**s** (these are the only German nouns which do not have their dative plural in -**n**), as with **das Hotel** (*hotel*), thus:

	Singular	Plural	Singular	Plural
Nom.	die Löwin	die Löwinnen	das Hotel	die Hotels
Acc.	die Löwin	die Löwinnen	das Hotel	die Hotels
Gen.	der Löwin	der Löwinnen	des Hotels	der Hotels
Dat.	der Löwin	den Löwinnen	dem Hotel	den Hotels

Common nouns which decline like this include:

(a) -in words: die Ärztin (*woman doctor*), die Engländerin (*Englishwoman*), die Französin (*Frenchwoman*), die Freundin (*female friend*), die Füchsin (*vixen*), die Hündin (*bitch*), die Lehrerin (*schoolmistress*), die Patientin (*female patient*), die Schülerin (*schoolgirl*) and die Studentin (*female student*);

(b) foreign words with -s plurals: das Auto (*automobile*), das Büro (*office*), das Café (*café*), der Chef (*boss*), der Park (*park*), das Radio (*radio*), das Restaurant (*restaurant*), der Scheck (*cheque*), der Streik (*strike*) and der Tee (*tea*).

Mixed declensions

The term 'mixed declension' is applied to a relatively small number of nouns which are strong (i.e. have genitive singular in -(e)s) but in the plural are weak (all endings in -n), as with **der Schmerz** (*pain*) and **der Name** (*name*):

	Singular	Plural	Singular	Plural
Nom.	der Schmerz	die Schmerzen	der Name	die Namen
Acc.	den Schmerz	die Schmerzen	den Namen	die Namen
Gen.	des Schmerzes	der Schmerzen	des Namens	der Namen
Dat.	dem Schmerz	den Schmerzen	dem Namen	den Namen

Common nouns which belong to the mixed declension include:

(a) genitive in -es: das Auge (*eye*), das Bett (*bed*), der Direktor (*director*), das Ende (*end*), das Hemd (*shirt*), das Ohr (*ear*), der See (*lake*), der Staat (*state*), der Strahl (*ray*) and der Vetter (*male cousin*);

(b) genitive in -ens: der Buchstabe (*letter of the alphabet*), der Friede (*peace*), der Funke (*spark*), der Gedanke (*thought*), der Glaube(n) (*belief*), der Haufe(n) (*heap*), der Same (*seed*), der Schade(n) (*damage, misfortune*), der Wille (*will*) and das Herz (*heart*), which, however, has accusative singular das Herz. Many of type (b) may often be found with an -n on the nominative singular.

Note the following four golden rules already exemplified in the above tables:

1   An Umlaut can only be added to **a, o,** or **u,** never to **e** or **i.**
2   Feminine nouns never change or add any endings in the singular forms.
3   Except for plurals in **-s** (as with **das Hotel**) all nouns in German add **-n** to form the dative plural, unless the plural already ends in **-n.**
4   In the plural, the nominative, accusative and genitive forms of all nouns remain the same.

There remain a number of oddments, such as words occurring only in the singular: das Blut (*blood*), das Fleisch (*meat*), das Gold (*gold*), das Heu (*hay*), das Mehl (*flour*) and das Obst (*fruit in general*); or only in the plural: die Eltern (*parents*), die Leute (*people*), die Ferien (*holidays*) and die Geschwister (*brothers and sisters*); the extremely common noun **der Herr** (*gentleman*), which adds **-n** for the remaining singular cases but **-en** for all the plural ones; and the oddity **der Käse** (*cheese*), which adds **-s** in the genitive singular and **-n** in the dative plural but no ending in any other case.

The student noticing the optional **e** in some genitive singular endings will wonder when to use it and when to leave it out. The best advice is in general to leave it out, but it must be used with nouns ending in a sibilant (**-s, -sch, -z**), as the genitive **-s** would not otherwise be pronounceable: **des Glases, des Tisches, des Schmerzes.** Apart from these cases it is regarded as old-fashioned or literary, and is dying out. An even more old-fashioned phenomenon is the addition of an **-e** ending in the dative singular of some masculine and neuter nouns, e.g. **dem Manne, dem Kinde.** It is mentioned here because the reader may chance to meet it in print – there is no need to learn it.

The essential parts of any noun are the nominative singular, the genitive singular and the nominative plural: from these the full declension of any noun may be worked out, and they will be found on looking up the word in a good dictionary – look up *town* and you will find '**Stadt** *f.* (-; ⁻e)', which indicates that **Stadt** is feminine, makes no change in the genitive singular, and has the nominative plural **Städte.**

This chapter has classified German nouns into declension patterns, setting out twelve examples in full, giving ten further examples of each and giving a number of general rules which will be helpful in mastering this section of grammar. The next chapter will consider some noteworthy points concerning the usage of nouns in German.

5 The Use of Cases

The chief difference in the use of nouns between German and English is, of course, the necessity in German of knowing which case of the noun is required. Since in English there is no difference in form between the nominative and the accusative, the rule that the subject comes first is almost absolute, and is the sole indication of the important difference between *The King kicks the Queen* and *The Queen kicks the King*. In German, however, it is possible to vary the order and say, for example, **Den Salat hat dieser Herr bestellt** (*This gentleman ordered the salad*) – the meaning is perfectly clear, and no-one will think that the salad ordered the gentleman.

With verbs which take a **complement** and not a direct object, that is to say verbs where the predicate is in fact the same as the subject, as in *He seems a nice man*, the complement will be in the nominative case, although in the position where English would expect the object. The commonest of these verbs are **sein** (*to be*), **werden** (*to become*), **bleiben** (*to remain*), **heißen** (*to be called*) and **scheinen** (*to seem*).

Mein Bruder **ist** ein guter Arzt. *My brother is a good doctor.*

Sein Sohn **wurde** ein berühmter Schauspieler. *His son became a famous actor.*

Er **bleibt** vorläufig ein freier Mann. *He remains a free man for the time being.*

Mein Lehrer **heißt** Herr Fischer. *My teacher is called Mr Fischer.*

Das **scheint** ein guter Vorschlag zu sein. *That seems to be a good suggestion.*

A noun placed alongside another to qualify it is said to be in **apposition,** and in German it must agree in case with the noun it qualifies:

Unsere Tante, die Ärztin, wohnt in Berlin. *Our aunt, the doctor, lives in Berlin.*

Ich gab es **meinem Freund, dem Lehrer**. *I gave it to my friend, the teacher.*

Ein Werk **ihres Sohns, des Komponisten** *A work by her son, the composer*

Note that words in apposition are always separated by commas in German and not just sometimes, as in English:

Ludwig der Zweite, König von Bayern, starb 1886. *Ludwig II, King of Bavaria, died in 1886.*

If the phrase in apposition, however, is the title of a book or journal, the rule concerning agreement of case lapses:

In **der Zeitung 'Die Zeit'** *In the newspaper 'Die Zeit'*

In **dem Drama 'Die Physiker'** *In the play 'The Physicists'*

Masculine and neuter nouns denoting quantity, weight, measure or value, and following a number expression do not take the plural form, and the noun denoting the thing quantified is invariable and not in the genitive as in English (where we have *of*):

drei Glas Bier *three glasses of beer*

drei Stück Kuchen *three pieces of cake*

sechs Grad Kälte *six degrees of frost*

zwei Paar Schuhe *two pairs of shoes*

drei Pfund Mehl *three pounds of flour*

zwei Kilo Äpfel *two kilos of apples*

BUT sechs Flaschen Wein *six bottles of wine*

vier Tassen Kaffee *four cups of coffee*

because **Flasche** and **Tasse** are feminine.

Another instance where English uses *of*, but German leaves the word in apposition without even declining it is with place names, when the place name is preceded by a common noun defining it, as in

die Stadt München *the town of Munich* die Insel Capri *the Isle of Capri*

am Rande der Stadt München *on the edge of the town of Munich*

Madrid ist die Hauptstadt des Königreichs Spanien. *Madrid is the capital of the kingdom of Spain.*

An instance where English has a complement, but German uses an accusative, is with the expression for *there is* or *there are* – **es gibt**:

Es gibt **keinen** Ersatz dafür. *There's no substitute for it.*

Es gibt doch **einen** Ausweg. *There is a way out, however.*

Other instances where German uses the **accusative**, perhaps surprisingly from an English point of view, are in expressions of time and in expressions of weight, value and space:

Er war **einen** Monat in London.   *He was in London for a month.*

Ich habe **den** ganzen Morgen gearbeitet.   *I've worked all morning.*

Ich bleibe nicht **einen** Tag länger.   *I shan't stay a single day longer.*

Einen Moment, bitte.   *One moment, please.*

Das ist **keinen** Pfennig wert.   *That's not worth a penny.*

Ich ging noch **einen** Kilometer.   *I walked a kilometre further.*

Dieser Sack wiegt **einen** Zentner.   *This sack weighs a hundredweight.*

The verbs **kosten** (*to cost*) and **lehren** (*to teach*) take two accusatives:

Das hat **mich einen** Haufen Geld gekostet.   *That cost me a pile of money.*

Er lehrt **sie die** erste Regel.   *He teaches her the first rule.*

A noun in the **genitive** case will usually follow the noun it qualifies, unless the genitive refers to a member of one's family or is a person's name:

das Buch mein**es** Freund**es**   *my friend's book*

die Wohnung sein**es** Bruders   *his brother's apartment*

die Mutter mein**er** Freundin   *my girl friend's mother*

das Haus ihr**es** Onkels   *her uncle's house*

die Schüssel **des** Hund**es**   *the dog's bowl*

BUT Peters Fahrrad   *Peter's bicycle*

Onkel Wilhelms Auto   *Uncle William's car*

Vaters Schreibmaschine ist auf dem Schreibtisch.   *Father's typewriter is on the desk.*

Although expressions of time are usually in the accusative, as mentioned earlier, if the expression refers to habitual or indefinite time the genitive is used:

eines Tages *one day*   eines Abends *one evening*

eines Sonntags *one Sunday*

morgens *in the morning*   nachts *at night*

sonntags *on Sundays*

Note that when the article is omitted, the word functions as an adverb and is therefore written with a small letter:

Ich spiele des **Abends** gern Karten.   *I like playing cards in the evening.*

BUT Meine Eltern machten **samstags** einen Spaziergang im Park.   *My parents used to go for a walk in the park on Saturdays.*

Mention was made in Chapter 2 of the adverbial genitive:

> Er verabschiedete sich leichten Herzens. *He took his leave with a light heart.*

In this construction the genitive corresponds to an adverbial phrase in English, often but not always with the preposition *of*, hence its being called an adverbial genitive:

> Er ging schweigend seines Weges. *He went on his way without speaking.*

> Das ist meines Erachtens kein Fehler. *That is not a mistake in my opinion.*

> Ich fahre immer zweiter Klasse. *I always travel second class.*

> Unter Menschen guten Willens erwartet man so etwas nicht. *One doesn't expect such a thing among men of good will.*

The basic use of the **dative** case – for an indirect object – corresponds to an English phrase with *to*:

> Ich gab **dem** Lehrer das Buch. *I gave the book to the teacher.*

but it is also used where English would have *for* or *from*:

> Sie füllte **mir** das Glas. *She filled my glass for me.*

> Jürgen hat **mir** Geld gestohlen. *Jürgen stole some money from me.*

This is known as the dative of advantage (or, as the case may be, disadvantage), and is akin to many other applications of the dative:

> Ich stehe meinen Kollegen **zur** Verfügung. *I am at my colleagues' disposal.*

> Ein Jahr darauf starb **ihm** die Frau. *A year later his wife died.*

> Wie geht es deinem Vater? *How is your father* (literally: *How goes it with your father?*)

It was mentioned in Chapter 1 that prepositions govern particular cases, and that certain verbs govern the dative or genitive case: it will be more appropriate to leave these points to be dealt with in the subsequent chapters to be devoted to prepositions and verbs respectively.

Finally there is the problem of distinguishing nouns which are identical in the singular form but have different meanings, different plurals and even different genders. We are familiar in English with nouns having identical form but different meanings – one need only think of the various meanings of 'chest', 'note', 'table' or 'watch' – but in German each meaning goes with a particular plural form or gender or both. Here are the commonest nouns which share the same gender but have two plural forms, depending on which meaning is being used:

das Band, die Bande *bond*

die Bank, die Bänke *bench*

die Mutter, die Mütter *mother*

der Strauß, die Sträuße *bunch of flowers*

das Tuch, die Tuche *kinds of cloths*

das Wort, die Worte *connected words*

der Zoll, die Zölle *customs duty*

das Band, die Bänder *ribbon*

die Bank, die Banken *bank*

die Mutter, die Muttern *screw-nut*

der Strauß, die Strauße *ostrich*

das Tuch, die Tücher *scarf, duster*

das Wort, die Wörter *unconnected words*

der Zoll, die Zoll *inch*

The commonest words which have different genders as well as, more often than not, different plural forms, are:

der Band, die Bände *volume, book*

der Gehalt, die Gehalte *content, capacity*

der Hut, die Hüte *hat*

der Kiefer, die Kiefer *jaw*

der Kunde, die Kunden *customer*

der Leiter, die Leiter *manager*

der Messer, die Messer *surveyor, gauge*

der Moment, die Momente *moment*

der Schild, die Schilde *shield*

der See, die Seen *lake*

die Steuer, die Steuern *tax*

der Stift, die Stifte *peg, pencil*

der Tor, die Toren *fool*

der Verdienst (no pl.) *earnings*

das Band, die Bande *or* die Bänder *bond/ribbon*

das Gehalt, die Gehälter *salary*

die Hut (no pl.) *protection, guard*

die Kiefer, die Kiefern *pine tree*

die Kunde (no pl.) *news, tidings*

die Leiter, die Leitern *ladder*

das Messer, die Messer *knife*

das Moment, die Momente *momentum, factor*

das Schild, die Schilder *signboard*

die See, die Seen *sea*

das Steuer, die Steuer *steering wheel*

das Stift, die Stifte *institution, home*

das Tor, die Tore *gate, goal*

das Verdienst, die Verdienste *merit*

These are the most obvious problem areas concerning the use of nouns and their cases in German. In the following chapter we shall turn our attention to adjectives.

6 The Declension of Adjectives

Adjectives are words which describe nouns, and when they come immediately before the noun, i.e. when they form part of the noun phrase which is the subject or object of the sentence, they must agree with the noun in number, gender and case. In other words they decline. In this position they are called **attributive adjectives**. When they occur within the predicate of the sentence and not immediately before the noun they are invariable and do not decline. These are called **predicative adjectives**. Compare **der junge Mann** (*the young man*) with **der Mann ist jung** (*the man is young*).

As with nouns, adjectives may have a weak, mixed or strong declension, but fortunately these are all quite regular and there are no exceptions. There are therefore only three sets of endings to learn, which in fact coincide in most cases between the three declensions, and are already familiar from the preceding chapters. The weak declension is used after '**der** words', the mixed declension after '**mein** words', and the strong declension where there is no '**der**' or '**mein**' word before the adjective. We shall first set out the three declensions in full, and then compare the adjective endings diagrammatically, to see how far they coincide, in order to indicate the minority of cases which are different and hence need closer attention.

		WEAK DECLENSION					
		Singular					
Nom.	der	neue	Lehrer	die neue	Rose	das neue	Buch
Acc.	den	neuen	Lehrer	die neue	Rose	das neue	Buch
Gen.	des	neuen	Lehrers	der neuen	Rose	des neuen	Buchs
Dat.	dem	neuen	Lehrer	der neuen	Rose	dem neuen	Buch
		Plural					
Nom.	die	neuen	Lehrer	die neuen	Rosen	die neuen	Bücher
Acc.	die	neuen	Lehrer	die neuen	Rosen	die neuen	Bücher
Gen.	der	neuen	Lehrer	der neuen	Rosen	der neuen	Bücher
Dat.	den	neuen	Lehrern	den neuen	Rosen	den neuen	Büchern

MIXED DECLENSION								
Singular								
Nom.	mein	alter	Freund	meine	alte	Tante	mein	altes	Haus
Acc.	meinen	alten	Freund	meine	alte	Tante	mein	altes	Haus
Gen.	meines	alten	Freundes	meiner	alten	Tante	meines	alten	Hauses
Dat.	meinem	alten	Freund	meiner	alten	Tante	meinem	alten	Haus
Plural								
Nom	meine	alten	Freunde	meine	alten	Tanten	meine	alten	Häuser
Acc	meine	alten	Freunde	meine	alten	Tanten	meine	alten	Häuser
Gen	meiner	alten	Freunde	meiner	alten	Tanten	meiner	alten	Häuser
Dat	meinen	alten	Freunden	meinen	alten	Tanten	meinen	alten	Häuser

STRONG DECLENSION						
Singular						
Nom.	schöner	Wein	schöne	Stadt	schönes	Beispiel
Acc.	schönen	Wein	schöne	Stadt	schönes	Beispiel
Gen.	schönen	Weins	schöner	Stadt	schönen	Beispiels
Dat.	schönem	Wein	schöner	Stadt	schönem	Beispiel
Plural						
Nom.	schöne	Weine	schöne	Städte	schöne	Beispiele
Acc.	schöne	Weine	schöne	Städte	schöne	Beispiele
Gen.	schöner	Weine	schöner	Städte	schöner	Beispiele
Dat.	schönen	Weinen	schönen	Städten	schönen	Beispielen

The above three declensions comprise altogether seventy-two examples, but it is immediately obvious that there are in fact very few different endings to learn: by far the commonest adjective ending is -en, accounting for no fewer than forty-four of the seventy-two cases, while the ending -e accounts for a further fifteen. It is a useful aid to learning to set out as a diagram just the adjective endings themselves, similar to the one overleaf, as the learner can then readily perceive that a certain pattern emerges, which should be committed to memory.

It is worth noting that the strong adjective endings are identical with the endings of **dieser, jeder**, etc., with the exception of the masculine and neuter genitive singular, where they have -en instead of -es. The weak and mixed declensions have -en everywhere except in the nominative singular (all genders) and the feminine and neuter accusative singular. Thus the weak/mixed endings may be collectively presented as follows:

	Singular			**Plural**		
	Masc.	*Fem.*	*Neut.*	*Masc.*	*Fem.*	*Neut.*
Nom.	-e/-er	-e	-e/-es	-en	-en	-en
Acc.	-en	-e	-e/-es	-en	-en	-en
Gen.	-en	-en	-en	-en	-en	-en
Dat.	-en	-en	-en	-en	-en	-en

It can be seen at a glance that three quarters of the whole table consists of the ending -**en** and that of the five cases which do not, only three differ as between the weak and the mixed declensions, so that if the learner remembers as a working rule that attributive adjectives end in *-en*, the number of exceptions to which special care and attention must be paid is very small.

A great many of the adjectives one meets or needs to use will be in the predicative position and will need no ending at all. A few examples:

Mein Haar ist **weiß** wie Schnee.   *My hair is white as snow.*

Heute ist sie sehr **krank**.   *Today she is very ill.*

Der Brief ist **lang** und **interessant**.   *The letter is long and interesting.*

Er wird **alt**.   *He is getting old.*

There is one category of adjectives which is invariable in the attributive position. These adjectives are formed from place names by adding -**er**. They have a capital letter:

Ich kenne den Stuttgart**er** Bahnhof.   *I know Stuttgart station.*

Ich esse eine Schwarzwäld**er** Kirschtorte.   *I am eating a Black Forest gateau.*

Ich lese jeden Tag eine Berlin**er** Zeitung.   *I read a Berlin newspaper every day.*

Any adjective may be used as a noun, in which case it will be written with a capital letter, and will follow the weak, mixed or strong declension according to whether it is preceded by a '**der** word', a '**mein** word' or neither. In other words it will decline exactly as though it were an adjective followed by a noun – in many cases there could be said to be the word **Mann** or **Frau** understood, which overrides the rule that other parts of speech when used as nouns are always neuter:

Der **Fremde** sagte nichts.   *The stranger said nothing.*

Ein **Fremder** steht draußen.   *There is a stranger standing outside.*

Ich habe **Verwandte** zu Besuch. *I have relatives visiting.*

Sie ist eine alte **Bekannte** von uns. *She is an old acquaintance of ours.*

Wir ehren das **Gute**, das **Wahre** und das **Schöne**. *We honour the good, the true and the beautiful.*

A particularly frequent use of the adjective as a noun is after **etwas** *something*, **nichts** *nothing*, **viel** *much* and **wenig** *little*:

Ich brauche etwas **Kaltes** zu trinken. *I need something cold to drink.*

Ich habe nichts **Neues** dort gefunden. *I found nothing new there.*

Ich habe viel **Gutes** von ihm gehört. *I've heard lots of good things about him.*

Er hat wenig **Interessantes** zu sagen. *He has little of interest to say.*

These, of course, follow the strong declension (having no 'der word' or 'mein word'), but the word **alle** (*all*) is a special case: a demonstrative or possessive adjective after **alle** will have the same ending as **alle**, but any other adjective will have -**en**, thus:

Nom.	alle seine	alten Freunde
Acc.	alle seine	alten Freunde
Gen.	aller seiner	alten Freunde
Dat.	allen seinen	alten Freunden

Moreover, when **alles** (*everything*) is followed by an adjective used as a noun, the adjective will have a weak ending, not as after **etwas, nichts, viel** and **wenig** above:

Wir wünschen dir alles **Gute**! *We wish you all the best*!

Wir werden alles **Mögliche** versuchen. *We shall try everything possible.*

Adjectives ending in -**el** drop the **e** when they are declined (cf. **unser, euer**):

Die Nacht ist dunkel. *The night is dark.*

BUT Es ist eine dunkle Nacht. *It is a dark night.*

Das Bild ist nicht übel. *The picture's not bad.*

BUT Das ist ein übler Geruch. *That's a nasty smell.*

Sie ist edel von Natur. *She is high-minded by nature.*

BUT Das war eine edle Tat. *That was a noble deed.*

Adjectives of colour which are of foreign origin are described in most dictionaries and grammars as indeclinable. In practice, however, only **lila** *lilac* and **rosa** *pink* are truly so; **beige** is often used in inflected form, **creme** *cream* occurs only predicatively, and with **oliv** *olive* and **orange** it is advisable to add -**farbene** *coloured* and inflect normally:

> Sie trägt eine **rosa** Bluse und einen **lila** Rock.   *She wears a pink blouse and a lilac skirt.*
> Sie hat ein **orangefarbenes** Kleid.   *She has an orange (coloured) dress.*

The adjective **hoch** *high* is spelt thus only in the predicative form; when inflected the **c** disappears – **ein hohes Gebäude** *a tall building* or **die hohen Berge** *the high hills*.

The principle behind the differences in adjectives (though it no longer applies throughout as it did a thousand years ago) is that if the word before the adjective does not indicate the gender and case, then the adjective must perform this function: this is why the strong declension shows so much more variation than the weak.

In German a long adjectival phrase may be used between an article and a noun, where English would require a whole clause. The phrase will usually end with a present or past participle declined adjectivally, and is also known as the extended adjective:

> Der **von Ihnen geschickte** Stadtplan war sehr nützlich.   *The town map which you sent was very useful.*

Note that this construction rarely occurs in spoken German, but is of very frequent occurrence in journalistic, broadcast and commercial correspondence usage.

In this chapter we have met the three sets of endings an adjective before a noun may have, and learned the circumstances in which each set is used, also the important fact that an adjective not before a noun does not change. The use of adjectives as nouns has been explained, and four exceptional usages (**alle**, -**el** adjectives, foreign colour words and **hoch**) have been noted. In the next chapter we shall proceed to examine how adjectives are used when comparison is involved, when this is bigger than that, or the other is the biggest of all.

7 Comparison of Adjectives

In English, when we want to say that one person or thing has more of the quality indicated by the adjective than another person or thing, or has more than anyone or anything else, we use the endings -er or -est (with vowel modification where appropriate), e.g. pretty, prettier, prettiest, provided that the adjective is a short one. With longer adjectives we insert *more* or *most*, e.g. intelligent, more intelligent, most intelligent. The basic adjective is called the **positive** or simple form (all the adjectives met with so far have been in the positive form), the -er or *more* version is called the **comparative** form, and the -est or *most* version is called the **superlative** form. German behaves very similarly, but uses only the -er, -(e)st method, and never employs **mehr** or **meist** for this purpose:

Positive	*Comparative*	*Superlative*
neu *new*	neuer *newer*	der neueste *newest*
intelligent *intelligent*	intelligenter *more intelligent*	der intelligenteste *most intelligent*

The comparative and superlative forms decline exactly like simple adjectives, but we give the superlative form with a **der** because it never in fact occurs on its own.

The optional (**e**) in the superlative ending is used with adjectives whose positive form ends in **-d**, **-t**, **-s**, **-sch**, **-ß** or **-z**:

> rund *round* der rundeste   bunt *brightly coloured* der bunteste
>
> hilflos *helpless* der hilfloseste   rasch *quick* der rascheste
> süß *sweet* der süßeste   stolz *proud* der stolzeste

Exception: komisch *funny* der komischste

Some monosyllabic adjectives modify the vowel in the comparative and superlative forms. Nineteen of these are among the commonest words in German, three of which (**groß**, **hoch** and **nah**) will be found later in this chapter among the few cases of irregular comparison. Here are the sixteen regular ones with vowel modification:

alt	*old*	älter	der älteste	arm	*poor*	ärmer	der ärmste
dumm	*stupid*	dümmer	der dümmste	grob	*coarse*	gröber	der gröbste
hart	*hard*	härter	der härteste	jung	*young*	jünger	der jüngste
kalt	*cold*	kälter	der kälteste	klug	*clever*	klüger	der klügste
krank	*ill*	kränker	der kränkste	kurz	*short*	kürzer	der kürzeste
lang	*long*	länger	der längste	scharf	*sharp*	schärfer	der schärfste
schwach	*weak*	schwächer	der schwächste	schwarz	*black*	schwärzer	der schwärzeste
stark	*strong*	stärker	der stärkste	warm	*warm*	wärmer	der wärmste

Other monosyllabic adjectives do not modify the vowel. In addition to **bunt, rasch, rund, süß** and **stolz,** which have already been quoted, here are a dozen common ones:

blaß	*pale*	blasser	der blasseste	falsch	*wrong*	falscher	der falscheste
flach	*flat*	flacher	der flachste	froh	*happy*	froher	der frohste
kahl	*bare*	kahler	der kahlste	klar	*clear*	klarer	der klarste
knapp	*scanty*	knapper	der knappste	matt	*dull*	matter	der matteste
roh	*raw*	roher	der roheste	schlank	*slim*	schlanker	der schlankste
voll	*full*	voller	der vollste	zart	*tender*	zarter	der zarteste

Adjectives ending in **-el** drop the **e** in the comparative, but not in the superlative:

dunkel	*dark*	dunkler	der dunkelste	edel	*noble*	edler	der edelste
übel	*nasty*	übler	der übelste				

There are half a dozen adjectives which are irregular in comparison:

groß	*great, big*	größer	der größte	gut	*good*	besser	der beste
hoch	*high*	höher	der höchste	nah	*near*	näher	der nächste
viel	*a lot*	mehr	der meiste				
wenig	*little*	weniger	der wenigste				
OR							
wenig		minder	der mindeste				

When **weniger** is used as a comparative form it is indeclinable, as is also **mehr.**

Expressions of comparison usually contain the word *than* or *as,* which is **als** or **wie:**

Er ist zehn Jahre älter **als** ich.   *He is ten years older than I.*

Der ältere Mann ist so groß **wie** mein Vater.   *The older man is as tall as my father.*

Die jüngere Frau ist schlanker **als** Inge.   *The younger woman is slimmer than Inge.*

Note that the noun after **als** has the same case as the noun before it:

> Es gibt klügere Leute als diesen Polizisten. *There are cleverer people than this policeman.*
>
> Die Rose ist eine schönere Blume als die Tulpe. *The rose is a more beautiful flower than the tulip.*

The translation of *less, fewer, lesser* and *least* needs special attention:

(a) *less* and *fewer* are translated by **weniger**, which is indeclinable:

> Ich habe **weniger** Bücher als mein Vater. *I have fewer books than my father.*
>
> Er hat immer **weniger** Glück als sein Bruder. *He always has less luck than his brother.*

(b) *lesser* is translated by **kleiner** (literally *smaller*):

> Das wäre das **kleinere** Übel. *That would be the lesser evil.*

(c) *least*, when it means *smallest amount* is **wenigst**:

> Er hat das **wenigste** Talent. *He has the smallest amount of talent.*
>
> Peter hat das **wenigste** Geld. *Peter has the least money.*

When *least* means *slightest* it is translated by **mindest** or **geringst** (**gering** = *little*):

> Ich habe nicht die **mindeste** Chance. *I haven't the slightest chance.*
>
> nicht im geringsten *not in the slightest, not in the least.*
>
> Ich habe nicht den **mindesten** Zweifel. *I have not the slightest doubt.*

at least can always be translated by **wenigstens** (with an **s**):

> Dieses Auto kostet wenigstens 80 000 Mark. *That car costs at least 80,000 Marks.*

Note the idiomatic expression, confusing to many English learners, **nichts weniger als** *anything but*, as in, for example:

> Er ist **nichts weniger als** intelligent. *He is anything but intelligent.*
>
> Sie war **nichts weniger als** glücklich. *She was anything but happy.*

The absolute comparative of adjectives is a term used to describe a comparative adjective indicating not two things or people but simply a fair degree of the quality referred to, thus **ein älterer Herr** does not mean that the gentleman in question is older than any particular other gentleman but is simply 'an elderly gentleman' as we would say in English. Similarly **eine längere Fahrt** *a longish journey*, **seit längerer Zeit** *for quite some time now*, and **in jeder größeren Stadt** *in every town of any size*.

The best way to memorise which adjectives modify and which do not is to repeat aloud to oneself the positive together with the comparative. Simply learning a list of positive adjectives often does not work – one tends to go astray with the odd one – but to learn aloud **alt, älter,** etc. and **blaß, blasser,** etc. is a much more effective aid to the memory.

Adjectives in all degrees of comparison may be strengthened by preceding them by appropriate adverbs. Positive adjectives may be strengthened by **ganz** (*quite*), **höchst** (*highly*), **recht** (*really*), **sehr** (*very*) or **ziemlich** (*fairly*), though this last one is not exactly strengthening the adjective. None of these could be used before a comparative form, which, however, can be strengthened by **noch** (*still, yet*), **viel** (*much*) or **bei weitem** (*by far*). Superlative adjectives can be strengthened by the prefix **aller-** (*of all*). These are illustrated as follows:

Er ist **ganz** klug.   *He is quite clever.*

Das ist **höchst** unwahrscheinlich.   *That is highly improbable.*

Ich bin **recht** böse auf dieses Kind.   *I am very annoyed with that child.*

Manfred ist ein **ziemlich** guter Fahrer.   *Manfred is a fairly good driver.*

Diese Geschichte ist **noch** länger als die letzte.   *This story is even longer than the last.*

Dieses Buch ist **viel** teurer als jenes.   *This book is much dearer than that one.*

Sie ist **bei weitem** älter als ihr Bruder.   *She is older by far than her brother.*

Er ist der **aller**dümmste in der Klasse.   *He is the stupidest of all in the class.*

There are a few adjectives which are used positively but are comparative in form; they are used only attributively and do form a superlative:

der äußere	*outer, external*	der äußerste	*utmost, outermost*
der innere	*inner, internal*	der innerste	*innermost*
der obere	*upper*	der oberste	*uppermost, topmost*
der untere	*lower*	der unterste	*lowest, bottom*
der vordere	*front*	der vorderste	*front, foremost*
der hintere	*back, rear*	der hinterste	*backmost*
der mittlere	*central, medium, middle*	der mittlerste	*most central, middle*
der niedere	*low, inferior*	der niederste	*lowest, lowliest*

Das **äußere** Tor ist geschlossen. *The outer gate is shut.*

Er wohnt im **äußersten** Süden von Italien. *He lives in the extreme south of Italy.*

Die **inneren** Organe sind alle gesund. *The inner organs are all healthy.*

Er wollte seine **innersten** Gedanken aussprechen. *He wanted to express his innermost thoughts.*

Der **obere** Teil des Gebäudes brennt. *The upper part of the building is burning.*

Ich nahm das **oberste** Buch vom Stapel. *I took the top book from the pile.*

Ich kenne nur den **unteren** Rhein. *I only know the lower Rhine.*

Meine Wohnung ist im **untersten** Stock. *My flat is on the bottom floor.*

Die **vorderen** Reihen waren nicht besetzt. *The front rows were unoccupied.*

Wir waren in der **vordersten** Reihe. *We were in the front row.*

Die **hinteren** Plätze sind billiger. *The rear seats are cheaper.*

Wir sind in der **hintersten** Reihe. *We are in the back row.*

Der **mittlere** Knopf fehlt. *The middle button is missing.*

Diese ist vielleicht die **mittlerste** Partei. *This one is perhaps the most central political party.*

Sie war von **niederer** Geburt. *She was of lowly birth.*

Die **niedersten** Klassen leiden am meisten. *The lowest classes suffer the most.*

One final point: to translate the English *more and more* followed by an adjective, German uses **immer** (*ever*) plus the comparative form of the adjective:

Er wird **immer** reich**er**. *He gets richer and richer.*

Dieses Buch wird **immer** schwierig**er**. *This book gets more and more difficult.*

Having covered in some detail the formation and use of comparative and superlative adjectives, we shall in the next two chapters turn our attention to pronouns.

8 Pronouns

A pronoun is a word which stands in for a noun; in the sentence *He left the book on the table and it stayed there for days*, there is no need to repeat *the book*: the pronoun *it* does the job much more neatly. The use of pronouns in German does not differ enormously from what we are familiar with in English, but unfortunately there are a lot of them to learn. This is because there are half a dozen classes of pronoun – **Personal** (*I, you, us*), **Reflexive** (*themselves, myself*), **Relative** (*which, who*), **Interrogative** (*what?* whose?), **Indefinite** (*one, something*) and **Demonstrative** (*this, that one*). Much the most important and frequently occurring are the so-called personal pronouns (though they refer to things as well as persons), and we include here for recognition purposes the singular and plural familiar forms **du** and **ihr** (mentioned in Chapter 1), but do remember that these are used only when addressing family, intimate friends, children and other small animals. The normal word to use for *you* is **Sie**, always written with a capital letter in all its cases. In the following table the genitive forms have been included for the sake of completeness, but they are in fact extremely rare, as will be explained in the next chapter.

Personal pronouns

Singular

Nom.	ich *I*	du *you*	Sie *you*	er *he*	sie *she*	es *it*
Acc.	mich *me*	dich *you*	Sie *you*	ihn *him*	sie *her*	es *it*
Gen.	meiner *mine*	deiner *yours*	Ihrer *yours*	seiner *his*	ihrer *hers*	seiner *its*
Dat.	mir *to me*	dir *to you*	Ihnen *to you*	ihm *to him*	ihr *to her*	ihm *to it*

Plural

Nom.	wir *we*	ihr *you*	Sie *you*	sie *they*
Acc.	uns *us*	euch *you*	Sie *you*	sie *them*
Gen.	unser *ours*	euer *yours*	Ihrer *yours*	ihrer *theirs*
Dat.	uns *to us*	euch *to you*	Ihnen *to you*	ihnen *to them*

The accusative and dative forms of personal pronouns are used when these are the direct and indirect objects of the sentence respectively, as implied in Chapter 1. When the direct and indirect objects of a sentence are both pronouns, the direct object comes first, but when one is a pronoun and the other a noun, the pronoun comes first irrespective of case – incidentally, when both are nouns it is the indirect object which comes first!

Mein Vater ist auch Lehrer – kennen **Sie ihn**? *My father's a teacher too – do you know him*?

Haben **Sie den Brief**? Ja, ich habe ihn. *Have you got the letter? Yes, I have it.*

Das sage ich **ihr** immer. *I'm always telling her that.*

Ich gab **Ihnen meine alten Bücher**. *I gave you my old books.*

Er bringt **mir gute Nachrichten**. *He brings me good news.*

Sie schickt **es ihrem Freund**. *She is sending it to her friend.*

Wir gaben **es ihnen** letzten Montag. *We gave it to them last Monday.*

Heute schicken sie **es uns**. *They are sending it to us today.*

Ich gebe **meiner Frau den Ring**. *I'm giving the ring to my wife.*

Take particular note that **ich** does not always have a capital letter as *I* has in English, but only when it begins a sentence, and that *it* is not always **es** – it may be **sie** or **er** or **ihn** or even **ihr** or **ihm**, depending on the gender of the noun it stands for and its role in the sentence.

We saw in Chapter 5 that German uses **es gibt** where English would say *there is* or *there are*. **Es** is similarly used with the verb **sein** (*to be*) to represent the subject, which then follows the verb, and with which the verb agrees; **es** is also used as a complement to the verb *to be* where English would have *it's*:

Es ist meine Schwester. *It is my sister.*

Es sind meine Freunde. *It's my friends.*

Ich bin es. *It's me.*

Sind es Ihre Schuhe? *Are they your shoes*?

Reflexive pronouns

When the recipient of an action is also the doer of the action, e.g. *He hurt himself*, the verb is said to be reflexive (the action being as it were reflected back upon the doer), and the object pronoun is a reflexive pronoun. In German the personal pronouns are used as reflexives (sometimes accusative and sometimes dative – see examples) except in the third person singular and plural and the polite form **Sie**. For these cases there is a special reflexive pronoun **sich** (*himself, herself, itself, themselves, yourself, yourselves* – which of these meanings applies will of course be evident from the subject and the context.) In many cases where English uses a simple verb, German uses a reflexive verb if the meaning is in fact reflexive. In some instances, however, it is not immediately obvious that the meaning is reflexive, and these verbs must simply be learned as one goes along, e.g. **sich verabschieden** (*to take one's leave*):

Ich muß **mich** jetzt verabschieden. *I must take my leave now.*

In other cases the reflexive pronoun will be dative and not accusative for usually obvious reasons. Examples:

Ich muß **mich** schnell waschen. *I must take a quick wash.*

Ich muß **mir** die Hände waschen. *I must wash my hands.* (The reflexive pronoun is dative because the direct object of the verb is *hands.*)

Er hat **sich** verletzt. *He has hurt himself.*

Das kann ich **mir** vorstellen. *I can imagine it.* (The reflexive pronoun will always be dative with the verb *to imagine something.*)

Bitte setzen Sie **sich**! *Please sit down.*

Wir müssen **uns** beeilen. *We must hurry.*

The reflexive pronouns can also be used as reciprocal pronouns, i.e. to mean *each other*:

Ich glaube, Sie kennen **sich** schon. *I believe you know each other already.*

Wir haben **uns** schon früher gesprochen. *We have already spoken together.*

Relative pronouns

A relative pronoun is one which begins a relative clause, that is, a dependent clause beginning with *who, whom, whose, which* or *that*, e.g. *This is the book that she gave me, I saw the man who came today, That is the lady whose handbag was stolen* and *Here is the magazine which you were asking about.*

In English the relative pronoun can very often be omitted: one could just as well say *This is the book she gave me* or *Here is the magazine you were asking about*, but in German it must never be omitted, and the relative clause must always be separated by commas. The words used as relative pronouns in German are **der** and (much less frequently) **welcher**, and they follow their accustomed declension (i.e. like **dieser**) with two important exceptions: in the genitive singular both **der** and **welcher** become masculine and neuter **dessen** and feminine **deren**, and in the genitive and dative plurals they have genitive **deren** and dative **denen** and **welchen** (no deviation from the norm for **welcher** in this last case):

Das Buch, **das** ich lese, ist sehr lang.   *The book I am reading is very long.*

Der Freund, **den** ich besuchte, war krank.   *The friend whom I visited was ill.*

Die Blumen, **die** ich kaufte, waren schön.   *The flowers I bought were beautiful.*

Die Frau, **deren** Sohn ich kenne, hat mich besucht.   *The lady whose son I know visited me.*

Hier ist der Mann, **dessen** Haus ich kaufte.   *Here is the man whose house I bought.*

Die Leute, **denen** ich Geld gab, sind sehr arm.   *The people I gave money to are very poor.*

Interrogative pronouns

The interrogative pronouns, i.e. those which ask a question, are **wer** (*who?*), **was** (*what?*), **welcher** (*which?*) and the special construction **was für** (*what sort of?*). **Was** and **was für** do not decline, **welcher** declines like **dieser** throughout, and **wer** is as follows. Note that it has no plural form:

Nom.	wer?	*who?*
Acc.	wen?	*whom?*
Gen.	wessen?	*whose?*
Dat.	wem?	*to whom?*

Wer ist da?   *Who is there?*
Wen meinen Sie?   *Whom do you mean?*
Wessen Buch ist das?   *Whose book is that?*
Wem sagen Sie das?   *To whom are you speaking?*
Was sagen Sie?   *What are you saying?*
Welcher ist der Chef?   *Which is the boss?*
Was für ein Ding ist das?   *What sort of a thing is that?*
Was für einen Wagen fährst du?   *What sort of car do you drive?*

Indefinite pronouns

Many adjectives and adverbs may be used as indefinite pronouns, e.g. **alles, viel(e)** and **wenig(e)**; some are indeclinable and cause no problems, for example:

Ich habe **nichts** zu essen gehabt – bitte, geben Sie mir etwas!   *I have had nothing to eat – please give me something!*

There are three which can decline; **man** (*one*), **jemand** (*someone*) and **niemand** (*nobody*): **Man** may variously be translated as *one*, *they*, *you* or *people*, but has this form only in the nominative, using **einen** and **einem** in the accusative and dative:

> **Man** sagt, wir werden schlechtes Wetter haben.   *They say bad weather is on the way.*
>
> So etwas tut **man** nicht.   *One doesn't do things like that.*
>
> Wie schreibt **man** das auf deutsch?   *How does one write that in German?*
>
> **Man** weiß nie, ob er **einen** erkannt hat.   *You never know if he's recognised you.*
>
> Die Luft hier tut **einem** gut.   *The air here does you good.*

Jemand and **niemand** may have -**en** in the accusative and -**em** in the dative, but these are optional:

> **Jemand** hat die Tür geschlossen.   *Someone has closed the door.*
>
> Ich sehe **jemand(en)** draußen.   *I can see someone outside.*
>
> Ich werde es **niemand(em)** sagen.   *I shall tell nobody.*

In the last example, one could use **keinem** instead; in general it is advisable to omit the endings on **jemand** and **niemand**, but the genitive ending must be used:

> Ich höre **jemand(e)s** Stimme.   *I hear someone's voice.*

Demonstrative pronouns

All the 'der words' may be used as demonstrative pronouns:

> **Der** ist der richtige Mensch!   *He's the right man!*
>
> **Den** kann ich nicht leiden.   *I can't stand that man.*
>
> Ich hatte **dieses** vergessen.   *I had forgotten that.*
>
> **Jener** gefällt mir besser.   *I like that one more.*
>
> **Jeder** muß helfen.   *Everyone must help.*

These are the commonest pronoun forms; in the next chapter we shall learn more of how they are used.

9 The Use of Pronouns

Personal

Personal pronouns should not be confused with possessive adjectives; the latter are followed by a noun, the former are not, and they decline differently.

> **Mein** Bleistift ist rot.   *My pencil is red.*
> Dieser Bleistift ist **meiner**, der andere **Ihrer**.   *This pencil is mine, the other yours.*

The pronoun **es** has many uses which do not have English equivalents – in many cases **es** is needed in German where English has nothing at all:

> Wir gehen zu Bett, und du solltest **es** auch.   *We are going to bed, and you should too.*
> Bist du fertig? Ich bin **es**.   *Are you ready? I am.*
> Sie ist reich, du bist **es** nicht.   *She is rich, you are not.*
> Man sagt, er ist dumm, und er ist **es** bestimmt!   *They say he's dim, and he certainly is!*

It can act as an introductory word like English *There*:

> **Es** steht ein Tisch in der Ecke.   *There is a table in the corner.*
> **Es** war ein König in Thule.   *There was a king in Thule.*
> **Es** blies ein starker Wind.   *There was a strong wind blowing.*

and also as a sort of indeterminate object, omitted in English:

> Sie haben **es** gut!   *You are lucky!*
> Er meint **es** gut.   *He means well.*
> Er wird **es** weit bringen.   *He'll go far.*
> Ich bin **es** satt.   *I'm sick of it.*

Note also that **es ist** for *there is*, which is more precise than **es gibt**, can have a plural **es sind**, whereas one can't say **es geben**; **es gibt** serves for *there are*.

Reflexive

The reflexive form of the pronoun must be used after a preposition when the pronoun in fact refers to the subject:

> Er hatte kein Geld bei **sich**. *He had no money on him.*
> Sie schloß die Tür hinter **sich**. *She closed the door behind her.*

The dative reflexive pronoun is idiomatically used as a dative of advantage:

> Ich will **mir** den Wagen ansehen. *I'm going to have a look at the car.*
> Er steckte **sich** eine Zigarette an. *He lit a cigarette.*
> Ich dachte **mir**, daß . . . *I thought to myself that . . .*

Relative

When the relative pronoun *which* refers not just to the subject, but to the whole preceding clause, e.g. *He collapsed completely, which shocked me,* **was** is used:

> Sie kommt immer spät, **was** mich ärgert. *She always comes late, which annoys me.*
> Er erhielt den Führerschein, **was** mich erstaunte. *He got his driving licence, which astounded me.*

Wer and **was** can be used as compound relatives, combining subject and relative:

> **Wer** wagt, gewinnt. *Who dares wins.*
> **Was** ich hatte, war nicht genug. *What I had wasn't enough.*

Interrogative

Although the interrogative pronouns **wer?** and **was?** have no plural, they may be used as the complement of the plural of the verb *to be*:

> **Wer** sind diese Leute? *Who are these people?*
> **Was** sind diese Dinge? *What are these things?*

They may also be used in exclamations:

> **Wer** hätte es geglaubt! *Who would have believed it!*
> **Was** du nicht sagst! *The things you say!*

Indefinite

Many words which are used in other contexts as adjectives or adverbs can be indefinite pronouns, and by no means all of them were mentioned in the last chapter, nor can we attempt a comprehensive list here, but the following are the commonest:

> **Alles** ist fertig. *Everything is ready.*
> **Alle** waren da. *Everyone was there.*

Beide (*both*) is normally an adjective, but the form **beides** is common as a pronoun:

> Ich hatte einen Fahrplan und eine Karte, und habe **beides** verloren. *I had a timetable and a map, and I've lost both of them.*
>
> **Beides** ist möglich. *Both things are possible.*
>
> **Beides** sind Ausnahmen. *Both are exceptions.*

Except with **sind** or **waren** before a plural noun, **beides** always takes a singular verb.

Einer may be used as a pronoun, for example:

> Eine Tür war offen, und **eine** war zu. *One door was open, and one was closed.*
>
> **Einer** von uns ist schuldig. *One of us is guilty.*
>
> **Einer**, der ihn kennt, hat es mir gesagt. *Someone who knows him told me.*

Like several other pronouns, **einer** is often strengthened by the prefix **irgend**:

> **Irgendeiner** muß es gemacht haben. *Somebody or other must have done it.*
>
> **Irgendeiner** seiner Freunde wird Ihnen seine Adresse geben. *Any of his friends will give you his address.*

Some and *Others* may be rendered by **Die einen . . . die anderen**:

> **Die einen** sind zufrieden, **die anderen** nicht. *Some are content, others are not.*

or by **einige** (*some, a few*) . . . **andere**:

> **Einige** blieben die ganze Nacht, **andere** gingen nach Hause. *Some stayed all night, others went home.*

Einige in the plural is *some* or *a few*:

> Nur **einige** sind hier. *Only a few are here.*

As a neuter singular pronoun it means *a certain amount, a few things*:

> Ich hatte noch **einiges** zu tun. *I still had a few things to do.*
>
> Ich habe **einiges** gefunden. *I have found a certain amount.*

A few may also be translated by the indeclinable phrase **ein paar** (N.B. with a small *p*; **ein Paar** means *a pair*):

> Ich habe noch **ein paar** übrig. *I've still got a few left over.*
>
> Wir werden noch **ein paar** kaufen. *We'll buy a few more.*
>
> Sie kaufte **ein Paar** Schuhe. *She bought a pair of shoes.*

Jeder (*each one*), **mancher** (*many a*) and **mehrere** (*several*) may be used as pronouns:

>**Jeder** von Ihnen muß zehn Mark bezahlen. *Each of you must pay ten marks.*
>
>**Manche** wollten es nicht glauben. *Many people wouldn't believe it.*
>
>Ich hatte ihm **mehreres** zu sagen. *I had a few things to say to him.*

Solcher as a pronoun is rare, except in the expression *as such*:

>Die Stadt **als solche** ist uninteressant, aber die Lage ist ganz einmalig. *The town as such is uninteresting, but its setting is quite unique.*
>
>Ich bin nicht gegen die moderne Musik **als solche**, sondern gegen ihre Anhänger. *I am not against modern music as such, but against its fans.*

Welcher is used as a pronoun quite widely in speech, with the meaning of *some*:

>Hast du Zigaretten? Ja, ich habe **welche**. *Have you any cigarettes? Yes, I have some.*
>
>Ich brauche Geld – kannst du mir **welches** geben? *I need some money – can you give me any?*

Whoever or *Whatever* is rendered by adding **auch** or **immer** or **auch immer** to **wer** or **was**:

>**Wer** es **auch** getan hat, er hatte unrecht. *Whoever did it, he was wrong.*
>
>**Wer immer** das gesagt hat, es ist falsch. *Whoever said that, it's not true.*
>
>**Wer auch immer** es sein mag, ich bin ihm dankbar. *Whoever he is, I am grateful to him.*
>
>**Was auch** geschieht, du kannst auf mich zählen. *Whatever happens, you can count on me.*

Demonstrative

The use of **der** as a demonstrative pronoun is much more a feature of spoken than of written German, and in speech the pronoun is always stressed:

>**Der** ist billig. *That one is cheap.*
>
>**Die** ist schön. *That one is beautiful.*
>
>Möchten Sie **den** haben? *Would you like to have that one?*

When it does occur in print, it needs some indication of emphasis;

English would use italics, but German is still influenced by the fact that fifty years ago it used to be printed in Gothic type, rather like a sort of horizontal Chinese (perhaps that is a little exaggerated), in which an italic version could hardly be imagined, so emphasis was indicated by extra space between the letters, and you may still meet this in print, thus: D e r ist billig. D i e ist schön.

This usage of **der** may be strengthened by the addition of **da** (*there*) or **hier** (*here*): **Der da** ist zu klein. *That one is too small.* **Die hier** ist gut. *This one is good.*

The neuter dative **dem** is used as an indefinite demonstrative in the following expressions, which all mean more or less the same thing: Wie **dem** auch sei, Wie **dem** auch sein mag *However that may be*, **Dem** sei, wie es wolle *Be that as it may*. Note that the genitive **dessen, deren** is helpful in avoiding ambiguity:

Er verabschiedete sich von seinem Freund und **dessen** Schwester. *He took leave of his friend and his – i.e. his friend's – sister.*

Dieser as a demonstrative pronoun is often shortened to **dies** with the verb **sein** plus a noun:

Dies ist meine Schwester. *This is my sister.*

Dies sind meine Eltern. *These are my parents.*

With neuter nouns **dieses** is often shorted to **dies**: dies Buch *this book.*

The one is the compound word **derjenige, diejenige, dasjenige**, in the declension of which **der** has the definite article endings and **jenig** the weak declension:

Diejenigen, die am besten spielen, bekommen den Preis. *The ones who play best get the prize.*

It is felt to be, however, an ugly and rather pompous word, and should be avoided.

The same (one) is another compound, **derselbe, dieselbe, dasselbe**, where **der** has the definite article endings and **selbe** follows the weak declension.

Sie ist immer **dieselbe**. *She is always the same.*

Er sagt immer **dasselbe**. *He always says the same.*

Welcher is felt to be old-fashioned as a relative pronoun and should be avoided, though occasionally it is useful to avoid repeating *der*:

Ein Kleid, das ihr gehörte, **welches** sie aber nie getragen
hatte . . .   *A dress which belonged to her but which she had
never worn . . .*

In addition to its use as an indefinite pronoun (mentioned above),
welcher is, of course, widely used as an interrogative pronoun and
demonstrative adjective:

Welchen Wein willst du wählen?   *Which wine would you like to
choose?*

Diese sind zwei gute Mannschaften. **Welche** wird gewinnen,
meinen Sie?   *These are two good teams. Which will win, do you
think?*

and it is also used in exclamations:

Welcher Unterschied!   *What a difference!*
Welche Überraschung!   *What a surprise!*

The above examples cover all that is really essential knowledge in
the complex area of pronoun usage. This section on the noun and its
associates will conclude with an account of the German treatment of
numerals.

10 Numerals

There are two kinds of numbers: cardinal numbers, e.g. one, two, three, which indicate how many things, and ordinal numbers, e.g. first, second, third, which indicate the order in which things come. The first twenty cardinal numbers are:

eins	*one*	elf	*eleven*
zwei	*two*	zwölf	*twelve*
drei	*three*	dreizehn	*thirteen*
vier	*four*	vierzehn	*fourteen*
fünf	*five*	fünfzehn	*fifteen*
sechs	*six*	sechzehn	*sixteen*
sieben	*seven*	siebzehn	*seventeen*
acht	*eight*	achtzehn	*eighteen*
neun	*nine*	neunzehn	*nineteen*
zehn	*ten*	zwanzig	*twenty*

Notice that 13–19 are formed simply by adding **-zehn** except for **sechzehn**, which drops its **-s**, and **siebzehn**, which drops its **-en**. The formation of numbers after twenty is as follows:

einundzwanzig	*twenty-one*	vierzig	*forty*
zweiundzwanzig	*twenty-two*	fünfzig	*fifty*
dreiundzwanzig	*twenty-three*	sechzig	*sixty*
vierundzwanzig	*twenty-four*	siebzig	*seventy*
fünfundzwanzig	*twenty-five*	achtzig	*eighty*
sechsundzwanzig	*twenty-six*	neunzig	*ninety*
siebenundzwanzig	*twenty-seven*	hundert	*hundred*
achtundzwanzig	*twenty-eight*	hunderteins	*hundred and one*
neunundzwanzig	*twenty-nine*	tausend	*thousand*
dreißig	*thirty*	hunderttausend	*hundred thousand*

Notice that the ending -**zig** is simply added except for **dreißig**, **sechzig** and **siebzig**.

The two important differences of pattern between German and English numbers are firstly that German reverses the English order and says two and twenty, three and twenty, etc., and secondly that a number in German is always written as one single word, which may look cumbersome to us, but does not really make it any more difficult to say or use, e.g. **hunderttausend**. 347, for example, in German is **dreihundertsiebenundvierzig** – observe that the *and* is in a different place from what we are used to. A million is *eine Million*, which is always treated as a noun, written with a capital letter and not compounded with a following number: 3,400,879 is **drei Millionen vierhunderttausendachthundertneunundsiebzig**, but it is exceedingly rare to see or have to write such long numbers, and in speech one is not conscious of saying a word which would nearly fill a whole line! Two other differences concerning the writing of numbers in figures are important: where we use a comma to separate thousands from what follows, German simply uses a space, so that 10,000 is 10 000 in German; and where we use a decimal point, German uses a comma, so that 2.8 (*two point eight*) is 2,8 (**zwei komma acht**).

A hundred and a thousand do not usually have an indefinite article before them, unless one wishes to stress the fact that it is *one* hundred, *one* thousand, and may omit 'and' after them:

hunderteins   *a hundred and one*
tausendneunzig   *a thousand and ninety*

The form **eins** is used when counting or when no noun follows, otherwise a noun will of course take the form appropriate to its gender: *one car* is **ein Auto** and *one hour* is **eine Stunde**. When needed as a noun, e.g. *to throw a one* (at dice) it is feminine: *eine Eins werfen*, as are all the cardinal numbers except **das Hundert** and **das Tausend**. The word for *zero* or *nought* is also feminine: **die Null**. In the expression **ein oder zwei** (*one or two*), **ein** is usually uninflected:

Ich brauche noch **ein oder zwei** Blumen.   *I need one or two more flowers.*

You may often hear **zwo** instead of **zwei**; it is accepted usage in giving telephone numbers, for example, to avoid any phonetic confusion with **drei**.

All cardinal numbers may have a form in -**er**, the most frequent use of which is with reference to money and decades, though it has other applications.

Ein Mann in den Fünfzig**ern**.   *A man in his fifties.*
Ich war Schüler in den fünfzig**er** Jahren.   *I was a schoolboy in the fifties.*
Zwei Achtzig**er**, bitte.   *Two eighty pfennig stamps, please.*
Er gab mir vier Zehn**er**.   *He gave me four ten mark notes.*
Ein Vier**er**   *a rowing four*   Ein Acht**er**   *a rowing eight*
Note: when referring to coins, notes or stamps it is usual to omit the

word **Stück**, **Schein** or **Briefmarke** if it can reasonably be assumed that the context makes it clear what is referred to; the words **Zehner** and **Achtziger** will be masculine referring to coins or notes because **Pfennig** (*penny*) and **Schein** (*note*) are masculine, but feminine referring to stamps because **Briefmarke** (*stamp*) is feminine.

Zwei and **drei** may occasionally be found inflected, e.g. Das Zeugnis **zweier** Experten *The testimony of two experts*, Die Mutter **dreier** Jungen *The mother of three boys*, but one only needs a nodding acquaintance with these forms, which can usually be avoided, e.g. Die Mutter **von drei** Jungen.

In expressions of multiplication the verb is always singular, never plural as it often is in English, and the word **mal** (*times*) is written separately:

Zweimal *twice* BUT Zwei **mal** zwei ist vier *Twice two is four, Two twos are four.*

Der vier **mal** hundert Meter Staffellauf *The four by one hundred metres relay race*

BUT Ich habe das Buch **dreimal** gelesen. *I have read the book three times.*

The words which most commonly qualify cardinal numbers are **über** (*over*), **knapp** (*barely*) and **rund, ungefähr** and **zirka** (also spelt **circa** and abbreviated only as **ca.**), which all mean *about* or *roughly*:

Es kostet **rund tausend** Mark. *It costs about a thousand Marks.*

Ich komme in **ungefähr acht** Tagen zurück. *I'll come back in about a week.*

Er ist **zirka 1,80m** groß. *He's about six feet tall.*

Das hat mich **über hundert** Mark gekostet. *That cost me over a hundred Marks.*

Er ist **knapp zehn** Jahre alt. *He's scarcely ten years old.*

Ordinal numbers (first, second, third, etc.) are of course adjectives, and decline as such. For the numbers up to twenty they are formed by adding the suffix -**te** to the cardinal number, e.g. **der fünfte** (*fifth*), **der dreizehnte** (*thirteenth*), except for 1, 3 and 8, which are irregular as in English, and have **der erste** (*first*), **der dritte** (*third*) and **der achte** (*eighth*) respectively. **Der siebente** (*seventh*) is often shortened to **der siebte**.

Ich fahre **zweiter** Klasse. *I am travelling second class.*

Er lebte zur Zeit Heinrichs des **Achten**. *He lived in the time of Henry the Eighth.*

Wir fahren am **achtzehnten** Juli. *We are travelling on the eighteenth of July.*

The ordinals from twenty to a hundred are formed by adding the suffix -**ste** to the cardinal number, e.g. **der zwanzigste** *twentieth*, **der einunddreißigste** *thirty-first*, **der zweiundsechzigste** *sixty-second*, **der hundertste** *hundredth*; then it all starts over again with **der hunderterste** *hundred and first*, e.g. **die sechshundertzweiundsiebzigste Nacht** *the six hundred and seventy-second night*.

Fractions (of which we have already met **das Drittel** (*third*) and **das Viertel** (*quarter*)) are formed by adding **-l** to the ordinal number and are all neuter, with the important exception of **die Hälfte** (*half*). Whereas some fractions, most commonly **Viertel** and **Zehntel** (*a tenth*), may combine with a following noun to give, e.g. **eine Viertelstunde** (*a quarter of an hour*), **ein Viertelpfund** (*a quarter pound*), the translation of 'half' is rather more complicated. As a rule of thumb one may use **die Hälfte** for *half the* and **halb** for *half a*:

Ich aß **die Hälfte** der Apfelsine. *I ate half the orange.*

Ich aß **eine halbe** Apfelsine. *I ate half an orange.*

Er trank **die Hälfte** der Flasche. *He drank half the bottle.*

Er trank **eine halbe** Flasche. *He drank half a bottle.*

but **halb** in its various forms is the more common word, and *half a dozen*, for example, is **ein halbes Dutzend**; *in half of Germany* is **in halb Deutschland**, *half dressed* is **halb angezogen**, but *half of the girls* is **die Hälfte der Mädchen**. It depends on whether the nominal or the adjectival/adverbial aspect is being stressed (grammatically considered), but you may find that **Sprachgefühl** guides you more easily and painlessly.

Finally some miscellaneous but important points in the area of numbers. Telephone numbers are usually given in German in pairs of digits as follows: 862719 = 86 27 19, said as **sechsundachtzig siebenundzwanzig neunzehn**; 920133 = 92 01 33, said as **zweiundneunzig null eins dreiunddreißig**. The date on a letter usually appears in the form **9. März 1986**, though the old-fashioned form **den 9ten März** may still occur. Note that a decimal point indicates the ordinal: **der 5. November** is read as **der fünfte November**.

In telling the time note that the word **Uhr** (*hour*) is not declined and may be omitted: **Es ist ein Uhr** or **Es ist eins** *It is one o'clock*; **Es ist Viertel nach zwei** *It is quarter past two* or – more old-fashioned – **Es ist Viertel drei** (i.e. it is one quarter of the way to three). **Es ist halb neun** and **Es ist acht Uhr dreißig** both mean *It is half past eight* – note that in German *half nine* means halfway towards nine, i.e. *half past eight* and so on); **Es ist elf Minuten vor vier** *It is eleven minutes to four*;

Wir treffen uns um zehn nach drei *We'll meet at ten past three;* **Um halb eins** *at half past twelve.*

Twice, thrice, four times, etc. are indicated by the suffix **-mal** on the cardinal number: **zweimal, dreimal, viermal**, etc., but when the word **das Mal** (*time, occasion*) does not mean *times* it is written separately and with a capital letter:

Ich bin hier zum zweiten Mal. *This is the second time I have been here.*

The suffix **-fach** corresponds to the English suffix *-fold* after a cardinal number:

Die Preise sind aufs Zehnfache gestiegen. *Prices have risen tenfold.*

Ein vielfacher Millionär. *a multi-millionaire.*

fünffach vergrößert *magnified five times*

Note that **einfach** means *simple* and also *single* in eine einfache Fahrkarte *a single ticket.*

This concludes the treatment of the noun and its associates, and we now turn to the verb and its associates. We shall soon greatly increase our ability to form the whole range of sentences as we get to know more and more verbs.

PART TWO

The Verb and Its Associates

11 The Conjugation of Weak Verbs

Verbs are really the key words in the grammar of any language, since any proper sentence must contain a verb, and it is the verb which makes clear the relationship between the noun phrases in the sentence. The base form of any verb, the form under which it appears in any dictionary, is called the **infinitive**, and in German it nearly always ends in -**en**, e.g. **füllen** (*to fill*), **kaufen** (*to buy*). Notice that the English equivalent begins with *to*, which is the hall-mark of the infinitive form in English. This -**en** may be called the infinitive ending, and what comes before it is the verb **stem**, so **füll-**, **kauf-**, are stems on to which other endings will be added to form the various parts of the verb. The rule that German infinitives end in -**en** has as exceptions only verbs whose stem ends in -**el** or -**er** such as **lächeln** (*to smile*), **flüstern** (*to whisper*) and a tiny number of odd verbs such as **sein** (*to be*) and **tun** (*to do*) – in any case, *all* German infinitives end in -**n**. The list of all the possible endings which may be substituted for the infinitive ending -**en** constitutes the **conjugation** of the verb, corresponding to the declension of a noun.

Verbs in German, as in English, may be **weak** (the vast majority), **strong** (a significant minority) or **irregular** (a very small number). Weak verbs are verbs which retain the same stem vowel throughout, strong verbs are those which systematically change the stem vowel, and irregular verbs (which could be said to have a mixed conjugation, to use the term employed for a similar phenomenon in noun and adjective declensions) have some characteristics of each of the other two groups.

The form of the verb used to describe an action or happening will vary to some extent to indicate who or what is performing it (first, second or third person singular or plural – see Chapter 1), and also to indicate when, if at all, it is happening, e.g. in the present, the past or the future. The reason we add 'if at all' is because some verb forms, e.g. *I should die if that happened to me*, or *If that were so, it would be terrible*, do not in fact represent things really happening at all. These sets of person endings for present, past, etc. are called **tenses**, and may be divided into simple tenses, where the verb is only one word, e.g. *I fill, I filled*, and compound tenses, where the verb is more than one word, e.g. *I have filled, I had filled*. In the case of compound tenses an additional verb, in this case the verb *to have* is needed to form the tense. A verb performing this function is called an **auxiliary** verb, but it can also function in its own right in sentences such as *I have a headache, He has spots*.

To form the present tense of a weak verb, endings are added to the stem as follows:

leben *to live*			**warten** *to wait*		
ich	lebe	*I live*	ich	warte	*I wait*
du	lebst	*you live*	du	wartest	*you wait*
er, sie, es	lebt	*he, she, it lives*	er, sie, es	wartet	*he, she, it waits*
wir	leben	*we live*	wir	warten	*we wait*
ihr	lebt	*you live*	ihr	wartet	*you wait*
Sie	leben	*you live*	Sie	warten	*you wait*
sie	leben	*they live*	sie	warten	*they wait*

Most verbs, like **leben**, drop the **e** from the ending in the third person singular and in the second person familiar forms, singular and plural. Verbs whose stem ends in -**d**, -**t**, -**chn**, -**ckn**, -**dn**, -**fn**, -**gn** or -**tm** retain the **e** throughout like **warten**. Examples include **reden** *to talk*, **arbeiten** *to work*, **rechnen** *to calculate*, **trocknen** *to dry*, **ordnen** *to arrange*, **öffnen** *to open*, **regnen** *to rain*, and **atmen** *to breathe*.

This is the only form of the present tense in German, in contrast to English, which has a compound form (*I am living, I am waiting*) in addition to the simple form above, and uses it to express unfinished action as distinct from, for example, habitual action; *Today I am waiting until he comes* and *I wait an hour every Sunday* would be **Heute warte ich, bis er kommt** and **Ich warte eine Stunde jeden Sonntag** respectively.

The simple past tense (I lived, I waited) is more commonly, but less correctly, referred to as the imperfect tense in German, and its endings are very similar to those of the present tense, but with the insertion of a *t*, thus: -**te**, -**test**, -**te**, -**ten**, -**tet** -**ten**.

ich	lebte	*I lived*	ich	wartete	*I waited*
du	lebtest	*you lived*	du	wartetest	*you waited*
er, sie, es	lebte	*he, she, it lived*	er, sie, es	wartete	*he, she, it waited*
wir	lebten	*we lived*	wir	warteten	*we waited*
ihr	lebtet	*you lived*	ihr	wartetet	*you waited*
Sie	lebten	*you lived*	Sie	warteten	*you waited*
sie	lebten	*they lived*	sie	warteten	*they waited*

This tense, called **das Präteritum** (the preterite) in German, is used to describe not only completed actions – Ich wartete eine Stunde und ging nach Hause *I waited an hour and went home*, but also continuing or unfinished actions – Ich wartete schon, als sie kam *I was already waiting when she came*. The latter use (English *I was waiting* etc.) is called imperfect, which originally meant 'unfinished', but the tense in German has to serve for both the simple past (or preterite) and the imperfect in English, and is used for narrative and description as well as habitual or continuous action in the past. It corresponds therefore to a number of English forms:

Das Kind **spielte**, während seine Eltern **redeten**. *The child played while his parents talked./The child played while his parents were talking./The child was playing while his parents talked./The child was playing while his parents were talking.*

Das Kind **spielte** jeden Sonntag im Park. *The child used to play in the park every Sunday./The child would play in the park every Sunday.*

There are two very common compound tenses: the perfect tense and the future tense. The perfect tense is formed by using the present tense of **haben** as an auxiliary with the past participle of the verb, which is made by adding to the stem the prefix **ge-** and the suffix **-(e)t**, to give, for example, **gelebt, gekauft, gewartet, geredet**, thus:

ich habe gelebt	*I have lived*	ich habe gewartet	*I have waited*
du hast gelebt	*you have lived*	du hast gewartet	*you have waited*
er sie }hat gelebt es	*he she }has lived it*	er sie }hat gewartet es	*he she }has waited it*
wir haben gelebt	*we have lived*	wir haben gewartet	*we have waited*
ihr habt gelebt	*you have lived*	ihr habt gewartet	*you have waited*
Sie haben gelebt	*you have lived*	Sie haben gewartet	*you have waited*
sie haben gelebt	*they have lived*	sie haben gewartet	*they have waited*

Although the perfect tense is preferred for actions in the very recent past, it is to a large extent interchangeable with the simple past, and though the simple past is more used in north Germany than in southern areas, the perfect is the predominant past tense of German conversation, the simple past being more literary. In a sentence with a perfect tense, the past participle goes to the end, thus:

Ich **habe** es ihr gestern abend **gesagt**. *I told her so yesterday evening.*

Ich **habe** Ihnen das Buch letzte Woche **geschickt**. *I sent you the book last week.*

The future tense is formed by using the present tense of **werden** (*to become*) as an auxiliary with the infinitive of the verb, as follows:

	Singular		Plural
ich werde leben	*I shall live*	wir werden leben	*we shall live*
du wirst leben	*you will live*	ihr werdet leben	*you will live*
er, sie, es wird leben	*he, she, it will live*	Sie werden leben	*you will live*
		sie werden leben	*they will live*

In a sentence with the future tense, the infinitive goes to the end

Ich **werde** dich morgen **sehen**. *I shall see you tomorrow.*

Ich **werde** Ihnen das Buch nächste Woche **schicken**. *I shall send you the book next week.*

Note, however, that German very often renders a future meaning by a present form:

Ich bin um 2 Uhr wieder da. *I'll be back at 2.*

Ich rufe dich gleich wieder. *I'll ring you right back.*

Two other compound tenses are the conditional tense and the pluperfect tense. The conditional tense (*I should live, you would live,* etc.) is formed by using another tense of the auxiliary **werden** together with the infinitive of the verb, as follows:

Singular		Plural	
ich würde leben	*I should live*	wir würden leben	*we should live*
du würdest leben	*you would live*	ihr würdet leben	*you would live*
		Sie würden leben	*you would live*
er, sie, es würde leben	*he she, it would live*	sie würden leben	*they would live*

Like the future tense, the conditional sends the infinitive to the end:

> An deiner Stelle **würde** ich es nicht **machen**. *If I were you I wouldn't do it.*
>
> Ich **würde** lieber zu Hause **bleiben**. *I should rather stay at home.*

The pluperfect tense (I had lived, we had waited etc.) is formed by using the simple past tense of *haben* as an auxiliary with the past participle of the verb:

ich hatte gelebt	*I had lived*	ich hatte gewartet	*I had waited*
du hattest gelebt	*you had lived*	du hattest gewartet	*you had waited*
er ⎫	*he* ⎫	er ⎫	*he* ⎫
sie ⎬ hatte gelebt	*she* ⎬ *had lived*	sie ⎬ hatte gewartet	*she* ⎬ *had waited*
es ⎭	*it* ⎭	es ⎭	*it* ⎭
wir hatten gelebt	*we had lived*	wir hatten gewartet	*we had waited*
ihr hattet gelebt	*you had lived*	ihr hattet gewartet	*you had waited*
Sie hatten gelebt	*you had lived*	Sie hatten gewartet	*you had waited*
sie hatten gelebt	*they had lived*	sie hatten gewartet	*they had waited*

This tense is used to describe an action completed before another began:

> Ich **hatte** schon hunderte von Briefmarken **gekauft**, als er mir seine Sammlung schenkte. *I had already bought hundreds of stamps when he presented me with his collection.*
>
> Er **hatte** die Arbeit **gemacht,** aber der Alte hat nie bezahlt. *He had done the work, but the old man never paid.*

These are the basic six tenses of modern German, and this weak conjugation covers most of the verbs you will come across; the remainder will be presented in the following chapters.

12 Verb Usage

We have just been using several of the technical terms used to describe different parts of the verb, such as infinitive, conjugation, tense, auxiliary and past participle. These distinguishing terms are necessary because a verb is not simply one word but really a whole system. We have already seen that there are six basic tenses (there are in fact a few more to come, but of secondary importance), one or more of which will occur in virtually every sentence. What we have not yet considered is the extent to which a verb may function as another part of speech, as a noun or as an adjective (so that in learning a verb you are getting at least three words for the price of one!). This, together with one or two further technical terms we shall need, is the subject of this chapter.

An example occurred in Chapter 3 **Das Schwimmen ist sehr gesund**. *Swimming is very healthy*, where a verb was used as a noun, and it was stated that when other parts of speech are used as nouns they are invariably neuter. In fact any infinitive can be used as a neuter noun, and this usage is more common in German than in English, where, however, it can crop up: *To err is human, to forgive divine, To see him is to love him*. One reason for its greater frequency in German is that it is often used to perform the function of another English verbal noun, the *-ing* form in, for example, the following cases:

Ich habe Angst vorm **Fliegen**. *I am frightened of flying.*
Sehen ist **Glauben**. *Seeing is believing.*

It is, of course, always easily recognisable in German by having a capital letter, whether or not it is preceded by an article.

'Infinitive' obviously comes from 'infinite', meaning 'unlimited' or 'unbounded'. The 'infinite' parts of the verb, which include participles as well as the infinitive, are those which are not limited to, or bounded by, a particular number and person. A **finite** verb is a part of the verb which is limited to a number and person, e.g. **Ich lebe** *I live*, **Wir warteten** *We waited.*

In addition to the past participle (**gelebt**, **gewartet**) there is also a present participle, which in English always ends in *-ing*, and in

German is formed by simply adding **-end** to the stem, e.g. **lebend, wartend** *living, waiting*. Both participles may be used as adjectives, when they will decline if they precede the noun: das **geflüsterte** Wort *the whispered word*, ein **gefülltes** Glas *a filled glass*, meine **geehrten** Eltern *my honoured parents*, das **fehlende** Buch *the missing book*, die **lächelnden** Kinder *the smiling children*, ihre **wartenden** Freunde *her waiting friends*, BUT Die Arbeit war schon **gemacht** *The work was already done*, Das finde ich **erregend** *I find that exciting*.

An exception to the rule that past participles are formed by adding to the stem the prefix **ge-** and the suffix **-t** is the large number of verbs of foreign origin fairly recently introduced into the German language and given the infinitive ending **-ieren**: these all form their past participle by simply changing the final **-en** to **-t** without adding a **ge-** prefix. Here are the commonest ones: abonnieren *to subscribe*, diskutieren *to discuss*, gratulieren *to congratulate*, informieren *to inform*, interessieren *to interest*, kontrollieren *to check*, organisieren *to organise*, orientieren *to orientate*, passieren *to happen*, probieren *to sample*, produzieren *to produce*, rasieren *to shave*, regieren *to rule*, reparieren *to repair*, reservieren *to reserve*, spazieren *to stroll*, studieren *to study*, telefonieren *to telephone*, trainieren *to train*, zitieren *to quote*. Examples: Wir haben die Sache diskut**iert**. *We discussed the matter*. Der zit**ierte** Satz *The quoted sentence*, Die organis**ierende** Behörde *The organising authority*. All finite verbs must have a subject, which is the doer of the action, the person or thing the verb is limited to or 'about', but not all verbs need have an object, which is a person or thing on the receiving end of the action. Thus the verb **brauchen** *to need* requires an object; one cannot just say **ich brauche** without saying what it is you need, whereas the verb **gehen** *to go* does not require an object, i.e. one does not go a person or thing: Wir gehen jetzt. *We are going now*. Verbs which have an object are called **transitive**, and those which do not are called **intransitive**. If you look up a verb in a dictionary, the first information given after the headword itself is usually v.t. (verb transitive) or v.i. (verb intransitive). Most verbs are invariably one or the other, transitive or intransitive: **weinen** *to cry* – Das Baby weinte *The baby was crying* could never be used transitively any more than **sagen** *to say* – Er sagte nichts *He said nothing* – could be used intransitively. Some verbs, however, can be both transitive and intransitive (which the dictionary indicates by v.t. & i.); **fahren** *to drive*, for example, is usually intransitive, as in Ich fahre heute nach Hause *I am driving home today*, but may be transitive, as in Ich fahre einen Opel *I drive an Opel*; similarly **rudern** *to row* in Er rudert sehr gut *He rows very well* – intransitive, but in Wir rudern ein sehr kleines Boot *We are rowing a* *very small boat* – transitive. The importance of the distinction is clear if one tries to turn the sentence round so that the object becomes the subject of the sentence. This produces quite acceptable sentences in some cases – *Nothing was said by him, The Opel is driven by me, The very small boat is being rowed by us* – but the others are impossible: nothing gets cried, home today is not driven by me, and very well does not get rowed.

When the subject of a sentence is doing the action, the verb is said to be in the **active** voice, but when the subject is on the receiving end of, or suffering, the action, the verb is said to be in the **passive** voice. This is formed in German by the auxiliary **werden** plus the past participle, so one can make a passive equivalent of an active sentence by changing e.g. Ich ärgere meine Frau *I annoy my wife* to Meine Frau wird von mir geärgert *My wife is annoyed by me*. It is clear from the previous paragraph, however, that only transitive verbs can be made passive in this way: intransitive verbs have no passive. Since in a passive transformation the direct object of the active sentence (**meine Frau**) becomes the subject of the passive sentence, a sentence with no direct object cannot be put into the passive. The passive can be, and frequently is, avoided by other constructions which we shall come across in due course, and so it is given no very exhaustive treatment in this book, but do note that the auxiliary **werden** is not confined to the formation of the future and conditional tenses.

The passive emphasises the action rather than the resulting state; if one wishes simply to describe the latter, the verb 'to be' plus the past participle (as an adjective) is used. Compare:

Die Arbeit **wird** gemacht.   *The work is being done, i.e. it is going on now.*

Die Arbeit **ist** gemacht.   *The work is done, i.e. it is finished.*

Die Tür **wird** geöffnet.   *The door is (being) opened.*

Die Tür **ist** geöffnet.   *The door is open.*

The reader who has noted the frequency in our examples of obviously irregular forms of the verbs **sein** and **werden** and the number of irregular past participles may be doubting the statement in the last chapter that the vast majority of verbs are weak. It is worth pointing out at this stage that there have occurred so far in the book no fewer than thirty weak verbs, namely: arbeiten *to work*, ärgern *to annoy*, atmen *to breathe*, brauchen *to need*, ehren *to honour*, fehlen *to be missing*, flüstern *to whisper*, folgen *to follow*, füllen *to fill*, hören *to hear*, kosten *to cost*, lächeln *to smile*, leben *to live*, lehren *to teach*, machen *to do*, öffnen *to open*, rechnen *to calculate*, regnen *to rain*, sagen *to say*, schenken *to give as a present*, schicken *to send*, setzen *to* *put*, spielen *to play*, trocknen *to dry*, wagen *to dare*, wählen *to choose*, warten *to wait*, wohnen *to live, dwell*, wünschen *to wish*, zahlen *to pay* and zählen *to count*, so that together with the twenty verbs ending in **-ieren** you already have fifty weak verbs to practise with!

There is one verb in the above list, however, which is rather an oddity: you can't do a lot of practice with **regnen** *to rain*, because it cannot be used with any subject other than **es**, and incidentally nobody knows what the **es** refers to! Verbs like this, whose subject is indefinite or is not specified are known as **impersonal** verbs, and we have them in English too. Like German, we use *it* for various weather conditions:

> Es donnert. *It is thundering.*
> Es friert draußen. *It is freezing outside.*
> Es hagelt. *It is hailing.*
> Es schneit. *It is snowing.*

In these examples and in many other cases **es** is the equivalent of English *it*, but often the impersonal verb with **es** corresponds to the English *there*, as for example **es gibt** *there is, there are*, which we have already met, and similarly **es klopft** *there is a knock*, **es klingelt** *there is a ring* – these are not purely impersonal verbs like **regnen**, but personal verbs being used impersonally, so that one should distinguish between true impersonal verbs and impersonal constructions in German which are not impersonal in English; these are quite numerous: not only **es klopft** etc., but also **Es ist mir gelungen** *I succeeded*, literally 'It succeeded to me', **Es tut mir leid** *I am sorry*, literally 'It does sorrow to me', **Es freut mich, daß** . . . *I am glad that* . . . , literally 'It rejoices me that . . .' – one cannot say **Ich freue, daß** . . . , not forgetting the commonest one of all, **Wie geht es Ihnen**?, usually shortened to **Wie geht's**? *How are you?*.

In this chapter we have explained the contrasting terms finite/infinite, transitive/intransitive and active/passive, and introduced impersonal verbs, as well as showing how parts of verbs may be used as nouns or adjectives. We have incidentally recapitulated all the weak verbs which have appeared up to this point, and introduced a new class of weak verbs, those ending in **-ieren**. Before proceeding to the conjugation of strong verbs, we shall consider more closely the three important verbs which serve as auxiliaries, and which are all to a greater or lesser extent irregular: **haben**, **sein** and **werden**.

13 Auxiliary Verbs

Haben, **sein** and **werden** on their own mean *to have, to be* and *to become* respectively.

haben *to have*

PRESENT

ich habe	*I have*
du hast	*you have*
er ⎫	*he* ⎫
sie ⎬ hat	*she* ⎬ *has*
es ⎭	*it* ⎭
wir haben	*we have*
ihr habt	*you have*
Sie haben	*you have*
sie haben	*they have*

SIMPLE PAST

ich hatte	*I had*
du hattest	*you had*
er ⎫	*he* ⎫
sie ⎬ hatte	*she* ⎬ *had*
es ⎭	*it* ⎭
wir hatten	*we had*
ihr hattet	*you had*
Sie hatten	*you had*
sie hatten	*they had*

PLUPERFECT

ich hatte gehabt	*I had had*
du hattest gehabt	*you had had*
er ⎫	*he* ⎫
sie ⎬ hatte gehabt	*she* ⎬ *had had*
es ⎭	*it* ⎭
wir hatten gehabt	*we had had*
ihr hattet gehabt	*you had had*

FUTURE

ich werde haben	*I shall have*
du wirst haben	*you will have*
er ⎫	*he* ⎫
sie ⎬ wird haben	*she* ⎬ *will have*
es ⎭	*it* ⎭
wir werden haben	*we shall have*
ihr werdet haben	*you will have*
Sie werden haben	*you will have*
sie werden haben	*they will have*

PERFECT

ich habe gehabt	*I have had*
du hast gehabt	*you have had*
er ⎫	*he* ⎫
sie ⎬ hat gehabt	*she* ⎬ *has had*
es ⎭	*it* ⎭
wir haben gehabt	*we have had*
ihr habt gehabt	*you have had*
Sie haben gehabt	*you have had*
sie haben gehabt	*they have had*

CONDITIONAL

ich würde haben	*I should have*
du würdest haben	*you would have*
er ⎫	*he* ⎫
sie ⎬ würde haben	*she* ⎬ *would have*
es ⎭	*it* ⎭
wir würden haben	*we should have*
ihr würdet haben	*you would have*

Sie hatten gehabt *you had had*   Sie würden haben *you would have*
sie hatten gehabt *they had had*   sie würden haben *they would have*

Note that, apart from the irregular simple past and the forms **hast**
and **hat** in the present, these tenses are those of a perfectly regular
weak verb.

sein   *to be*

PRESENT

		FUTURE	
ich bin	*I am*	ich werde sein	*I shall be*
du bist	*you are*	du wirst sein	*you will be*
er ⎫	*he* ⎫	er ⎫	*he* ⎫
sie ⎬ ist	*she* ⎬ *is*	sie ⎬ wird sein	*she* ⎬ *will be*
es ⎭	*it* ⎭	es ⎭	*it* ⎭
wir sind	*we are*	wir werden sein	*we shall be*
ihr seid	*you are*	ihr werdet sein	*you will be*
Sie sind	*you are*	Sie werden sein	*you will be*
sie sind	*they are*	sie werden sein	*they will be*

SIMPLE PAST		PERFECT	
ich war	*I was*	ich bin gewesen	*I have been*
du warst	*you were*	du bist gewesen	*you have been*
er ⎫	*he* ⎫	er ⎫	*he* ⎫
sie ⎬ war	*she* ⎬ *was*	sie ⎬ ist gewesen	*she* ⎬ *has been*
es ⎭	*it* ⎭	es ⎭	*it* ⎭
wir waren	*we were*	wir sind gewesen	*we have been*
ihr wart	*you were*	ihr seid gewesen	*you have been*
Sie waren	*you were*	Sie sind gewesen	*you have been*
sie waren	*they were*	sie sind gewesen	*they have been*

PLUPERFECT		CONDITIONAL	
ich war gewesen	*I had been*	ich würde sein	*I should be*
du warst gewesen	*you had been*	du würdest sein	*you would be*
er ⎫	*he* ⎫	er ⎫	*he* ⎫
sie ⎬ war gewesen	*she* ⎬ *had been*	sie ⎬ würde sein	*she* ⎬ *would be*
es ⎭	*it* ⎭	es ⎭	*it* ⎭
wir waren gewesen	*we had been*	wir würden sein	*we should be*
ihr wart gewesen	*you had been*	ihr würdet sein	*you would be*
Sie waren gewesen	*you had been*	Sie würden sein	*you would be*
sie waren gewesen	*they had been*	sie würden sein	*they would be*

This is a much more irregular verb than **haben** – indeed, the verb *to be*
is the most irregular verb of all in many languages. Note that its
perfect and pluperfect are formed with **sein** as the auxiliary as well.

werden   *to become*

PRESENT		FUTURE	
ich werde	*I become*	ich werde werden	*I shall become*
du wirst	*you become*	du wirst werden	*you will become*
er	*he*	er	*he*
sie } wird	*she } becomes*	sie } wird werden	*she } will become*
es	*it*	es	*it*
wir werden	*we become*	wir werden werden	*we shall become*
ihr werdet	*you become*	ihr werdet werden	*you will become*
Sie werden	*you become*	Sie werden werden	*you will become*
sie werden	*they become*	sie werden werden	*they will become*

SIMPLE PAST		PERFECT	
ich wurde	*I became*	ich bin geworden	*I have become*
du wurdest	*you became*	du bist geworden	*you have become*
er	*he*	er	*he*
sie } wurde	*she } became*	sie } ist geworden	*she } has become*
es	*it*	es	*it*
wir wurden	*we became*	wir sind geworden	*we have become*
ihr wurdet	*you became*	ihr seid geworden	*you have become*
Sie wurden	*you became*	Sie sind geworden	*you have become*
sie wurden	*they became*	sie sind geworden	*they have become*

PLUPERFECT		CONDITIONAL	
ich war geworden	*I had become*	ich würde werden	*I should become*
du warst geworden	*you had become*	du würdest werden	*you would become*
er	*he*	er	*he*
sie } war geworden	*she } had become*	sie } würde werden	*she } would become*
es	*it*	es	*it*
wir waren geworden	*we had become*	wir würden werden	*we would become*
ihr wart geworden	*you had become*	ihr würdet werden	*you would become*
Sie waren geworden	*you had become*	Sie würden werden	*you would become*
sie waren geworden	*they had become*	sie würden werden	*they would become*

werden too forms its compound past tenses with the auxiliary **sein**, being one of a relatively small number of intransitive verbs which do so. They are mainly verbs denoting a change of place, such as ankommen *to arrive*, erscheinen *to appear*, fahren *to travel*, fallen *to fall*, fliegen *to fly*, folgen *to follow*, gehen *to go*, klettern *to climb*, kommen *to come*, laufen *to run*, reiten *to ride*, rudern *to row*, schwimmen *to swim*, stürzen *to rush*, treten *to step*, verschwinden *to disappear*, or else a change of state, such as einschlafen *to fall asleep*, entstehen *to come into being*, erschrecken *to get a fright*, heilen *to heal*, platzen *to burst*, schmelzen *to melt*, sterben *to die*, vergehen *to pass* (of time), wachsen *to grow*. Some of these verbs may be transitive or intransitive – only when they are intransitive are they conjugated with **sein**; all transitive verbs conjugate with **haben**. There are a few more verbs which take **sein**, most of them concerned with happening. They are begegnen *to meet*, bleiben *to remain*, gelingen *to succeed*, geschehen *to happen*, mißglücken and mißlingen both meaning *to fail*, passieren and vorkommen both meaning *to happen* and, of course, sein and werden.

When **werden** is used as an auxiliary to form the passive, as mentioned in Chapter 12, its past participle is **worden** and not **geworden**; the six basic tenses in the passive have the following pattern:

PRESENT   Ich werde geärgert   *I am being annoyed*

FUTURE   Ich werde geärgert werden   *I shall be annoyed*

SIMPLE PAST   Ich wurde geärgert   *I was annoyed*

PERFECT   Ich bin geärgert worden   *I have been annoyed*

PLUPERFECT   Ich war geärgert worden   *I had been annoyed*

CONDITIONAL   Ich würde geärgert werden   *I should be annoyed*

Remember that the simple past and the perfect are both used for a variety of English meanings: **sagte** may be *said* or *was saying*, and **hat gesagt** may be *said* or *has said*, and that the two tenses in German are more often than not interchangeable, so one need not worry. In Chapter 19 a class of words will be explained which can render the continuous aspect of German tenses. Finally, a reminder that the passive is needed mainly for recognition purposes, being much used in newspapers and in business and commerce. One rarely needs to use it oneself, as it is generally easier to use the indefinite pronoun **man** (*one*), which gives us sentences such as Man kauft solche Sachen auf dem Marktplatz *One buys such things in the market place* instead of the more cumbersome Solche Sachen werden auf dem Marktplatz gekauft *Such things are bought in the market place*.

Of the thirty or so common verbs conjugated with **sein** the great majority are strong or irregular verbs, and in the next chapter the conjugation of these will be set out.

14 Strong and Irregular Verbs

Strong verbs in German, as in English, are those which form the simple past tense not by adding -**te** (-*ed*) to the stem, but by changing the stem vowel. The past participle may have yet another stem vowel change, or may have the same stem vowel as either the simple past or the infinitive. In any case the past participle will end in -**en** and not in -(**e**)**t**. Clearly it is going to require a lot of hard work to familiarise oneself with the important ones, and unfortunately strong verbs can not usually be avoided as, for example, the passive construction can. Because these are the basic key verbs of the language, one cannot do without them. This has two advantages, however: they crop up so repeatedly in all German speech and writing that the opportunity for familiarisation is abundantly and rapidly available, and their counterparts in English are equally familiar and frequent in use, but one must be careful not to assume that the vowel pattern is always identical in German and English. This is indeed the case with **singen, sang, gesungen** *sing, sang, sung* but not with **finden, fand, gefunden** *find, found, found.* Each verb will have to be learned separately, but it will clearly be helpful to group together strong verbs which have the same pattern of vowel change, and they are so grouped in the list of strong verbs which constitutes Appendix III at the end of the book (pages 145–8).

It is customary to indicate the pattern of vowel change by listing the infinitive, then the third person singular present, then the third person singular simple past, and finally the auxiliary and the past participle, for example:

  laufen läuft lief ist gelaufen *to run*

You may sometimes find this abbreviated to

  laufen äu, ie, au, aux. sein *run*

These are called the principal parts of the verb, because a knowledge of these four parts will enable one to construct the verb's entire conjugation correctly. Here are the six basic tenses in full of **sehen (sieht, sah, hat gesehen)** – *to see*:

PRESENT		FUTURE	
ich sehe	*I see*	ich werde sehen	*I shall see*
du siehst	*you see*	du wirst sehen	*you will see*
er	*he*	er	*he*
sie } sieht	*she } sees*	sie } wird sehen	*she } will see*
es	*it*	es	*it*
wir sehen	*we see*	wir werden sehen	*we shall see*
ihr seht	*you see*	ihr werdet sehen	*you will see*
Sie sehen	*you see*	Sie werden sehen	*you will see*
sie sehen	*they see*	sie werden sehen	*they will see*

SIMPLE PAST		PERFECT	
ich sah	*I saw*	ich habe gesehen	*I have seen*
du sahst	*you saw*	du hast gesehen	*you have seen*
er	*he*	er	*he*
sie } sah	*she } saw*	sie } hat gesehen	*she } has seen*
es	*it*	es	*it*
wir sahen	*we saw*	wir haben gesehen	*we have seen*
ihr saht	*you saw*	ihr habt gesehen	*you have seen*
Sie sahen	*you saw*	Sie haben gesehen	*you have seen*
sie sahen	*they saw*	sie haben gesehen	*they have seen*

PLUPERFECT		CONDITIONAL	
ich hatte gesehen	*I had seen*	ich würde sehen	*I should see*
du hattest gesehen	*you had seen*	du würdest sehen	*you would see*
er	*he*	er	*he*
sie } hatte	*she } had seen*	sie } würde sehen	*she } would see*
es } gesehen	*it*	es	*it*
wir hatten gesehen	*we had seen*	wir würden sehen	*we should see*
ihr hattet gesehen	*you had seen*	ihr würdet sehen	*you would see*
Sie hatten gesehen	*you had seen*	Sie würden sehen	*you would see*
sie hatten gesehen	*they had seen*	sie würden sehen	*they would see*

It can be seen at a glance that so far as the future and conditional tenses are concerned, there is no difference between weak verbs and strong or irregular verbs, and obviously whether a strong verb is conjugated with **haben** or **sein** will only make a difference so far as the perfect and pluperfect tenses are concerned. These differences are as follows for a verb conjugated with **sein**, such as **gehen (geht, ging, ist**

gegangen) – *to go*:

PERFECT		PLUPERFECT	
ich bin gegangen	*I have gone*	ich war gegangen	*I had gone*
du bist gegangen	*you have gone*	du warst gegangen	*you had gone*
er sie ⎱ ist gegangen es ⎰	*he she ⎱ has gone it ⎰*	er sie ⎱ war es ⎰ gegangen	*he she ⎱ had gone it ⎰*
wir sind gegangen	*we have gone*	wir waren gegangen	*we had gone*
ihr seid gegangen	*you have gone*	ihr wart gegangen	*you had gone*
Sie sind gegangen	*you have gone*	Sie waren gegangen	*you had gone*
sie sind gegangen	*they have gone*	sie waren gegangen	*they had gone*

Irregular verbs, described above as having some weak and some strong characteristics, are few in number but frequent in occurrence, and may be put into two groups, one of which, the modal auxiliaries, will be dealt with in Chapter 16. The remainder have the endings characteristic of weak verbs together with the stem vowel change characteristic of strong verbs, for example **denken, dachte, gedacht** *to think*:

PRESENT		PERFECT	
ich denke	*I think*	ich habe gedacht	*I have thought*
du denkst	*you think*	du hast gedacht	*you have thought*
er sie ⎱ denkt es ⎰	*he she ⎱ thinks it ⎰*	er sie ⎱ hat gedacht es ⎰	*he she ⎱ has thought it ⎰*
wir denken	*we think*	wir haben gedacht	*we have thought*
ihr denkt	*you think*	ihr habt gedacht	*you have thought*
Sie denken	*you think*	Sie haben gedacht	*you have thought*
sie denken	*they think*	sie haben gedacht	*they have thought*

SIMPLE PAST		PLUPERFECT	
ich dachte	*I thought*	ich hatte gedacht	*I had thought*
du dachtest	*you thought*	du hattest gedacht	*you had thought*
er sie ⎱ dachte es ⎰	*he she ⎱ thought it ⎰*	er sie ⎱ hatte gedacht es ⎰	*he she ⎱ had thought it ⎰*
wir dachten	*we thought*	wir hatten gedacht	*we had thought*

ihr dachtet	*you thought*	ihr hattet gedacht	*you had thought*
Sie dachten	*you thought*	Sie hatten gedacht	*you had thought*
sie dachten	*they thought*	sie hatten gedacht	*they had thought*

Verbs having this mixed conjugation include **brennen, brannte, gebrannt** *to burn*, **bringen, brachte, gebracht** *to bring*, **kennen, kannte, gekannt** *to know*, **nennen, nannte, genannt** *to name*, **rennen, rannte, ist gerannt** *to run*, and two which may also be weak: **senden, sandte, gesandt** – or **sendete, gesendet** *to send*, and **wenden, wandte, gewandt** – or **wendete, gewendet** *to turn*. The irregular verb **wissen, weiß, wußte, gewußt** *to know* need occasion no confusion with its apparent synonym **kennen**: **wissen** is to know facts, while **kennen** is to know people or places. Examples: Ich weiß, was ich mache. *I know what I'm doing.* but Ich kenne sie seit Jahren. *I've known her for years.* Weißt du, ob er kommt? *Do you know whether he is coming?* but Kennst du meine Schwester? *Do you know my sister?*

A further irregularity in the conjugation of some strong verbs is that those which modify the vowel in the present tense and have a stem ending in -t add nothing in the third person singular and not -et as weak verbs do. Thus **halten** *to hold* has **ich halte, du hältst, er hält**; **raten** *to advise* has **ich rate, du rätst, er rät**; **treten** *to step* has **ich trete, du trittst, er tritt**; **fechten** *to fence* has **ich fechte, du fichtst, er ficht**; **gelten** *to be worth* has **ich gelte, du giltst, er gilt**; **braten** *to roast* has **ich brate, du brätst, er brät**; **flechten** *to twine* has **ich flechte, du flichtst, er flicht**; and **schelten** *to scold* has **ich schelte, du schiltst, er schilt**.

Note that when a verb is used reflexively (see Chapter 8), it will be conjugated with **haben** even if it is normally conjugated with **sein**, whether it is strong or weak:

> Wir haben **uns** müde **gelaufen**. *We've walked till we're tired out.*

> Die Wunde hat **sich geheilt**. *The wound healed itself.*

The only exceptions are sentences where the reflexive pronoun is not a true reflexive but a reciprocal pronoun meaning *each other*, e.g. Wir sind uns gestern auf der Straße begegnet. *We met in the street yesterday.*

There are no particular pitfalls associated with the use of strong and irregular verbs; the only problem is simply to learn their multifarious principal parts. It is recommended that the reader should try to memorise Appendix III one group at a time and not all at one go. Meanwhile another category of verbs must be considered: those formed with prefixes, which may be separable or inseparable, in some ways like such English verbs as *to undergo* and *to go under*.

15 Inseparable and Separable Prefixes

It is common to find in German, as in English, that a verb has several associated compound verbs which are formed by adding a prefix to it. In English we have, for example, *to take*, *to mistake*, *to overtake*, *to retake* and *to undertake*. As *take* is a strong verb, all its compounds likewise form their simple past tense and participle with *took* and *taken* respectively. Similarly in German the strong verb **schließen**, **schloß**, **geschlossen** *to close* has a number of compounds formed by adding various prefixes and all having the same strong conjugation, e.g. **beschließen** *to resolve*, **sich entschließen** *to decide*, **erschließen** *to open up*, **verschließen** *to lock*. There are nine prefixes in German which can be added to verbs in this way to form compound verbs. They are **be-**, **emp-**, **ent-**, **er-**, **ge-**, **miß-**, **ver-**, **wider-** and **zer-**. None of them exists as an independent word, they are always unstressed, and verbs which begin with any of them do not add the prefix **ge-** to form the past participle, thus: **beschließen**, **beschloß**, **beschlossen**; **verschließen**, **verschloß**, **verschlossen**, etc. Because they are never separated from the stem of the verb, they are known as **inseparable prefixes**.

Each of these inseparable prefixes tends to modify the meaning of the root verb in a consistent way, and this will be further dealt with later in this chapter; the most important points, however, are that these prefixes shift the stress on to the following syllable, and that they have no **ge-** in the past participle.

Other prefixes may be separable, that is to say that although in the infinitive form they appear as being part of the word, e.g. **ausgehen** *to go out*, the prefix operates separately in finite forms such as wir gehen aus *we are going out*, and precedes the **ge-** in the past participle (wir sind ausgegangen – *we went out*). These prefixes are much more numerous than the inseparable ones: the commonest are **ab-**, **an-**, **auf-**, **ein-**, **mit-**, **nach-**, **vor-**, **zu-**, **zurück-**, **zusammen-** and some which may be either inseparable or separable, **durch-**, **um-**, **über-**, **wieder-**; when separable these are stressed, and when inseparable they are unstressed, so that for example **abnehmen** *to take off* must be stressed on the first syllable, but **übersetzen** may be stressed on the first syllable if it is a separable verb, in which case it means *to ferry across*, as in Er hat uns in einem Boot übergesetzt. *He ferried us across in a boat.*, or on the third syllable if it is an inseparable verb, in which case it means *to translate*, as in Sie haben Kafkas Werke übersetzt. *They translated the works of Kafka.*

When the separable prefix is parted from the verb, as in wir gehen aus, it always occupies the final position in its clause. e.g. Sie **geht** jeden Abend um acht Uhr **aus**. *She goes out every evening at eight o'clock.*; in this regard German is less flexible than English, where one may say either *I'll take my coat off* or *I'll take off my coat*. The pattern with, for example, **zurückkommen** *to come back* is Ich **komme** bald **zurück** or Ich werde bald **zurückkommen** *I'll come back soon*; Ich **komme** in einer Stunde **zurück** *I'll be back in an hour*; Er ist nach einer Stunde **zurückgekommen** *He came back an hour later.*

When the infinitive of a separable verb is used with **zu**, the **zu** is put between the separable prefix and the basic verb, e.g. Er versprach, bald **zurückzukommen**. *He promised to come back soon.* cf. Er versprach, mich nach Hause zu bringen. *He promised to take me home.*

The commonest separable prefixes exist as independent words, usually prepositions, but there are many compound prefixes which may consist of a preposition with an adverb (in either order) and are in effect double prefixes. A second type of double prefix is formed by the combination of a separable with an inseparable prefix. German is very rich in the possibilities of forming such verbs, but suffice it to say for the moment that the former class of double prefixes mainly begin with **hin-** or **her-** (**heraus-**, **herum-**, **hinab-**, **hinauf-**, etc.), while the second class is best learned as each verb crops up, rather than setting out to collect them together, e.g. such verbs as **anerkennen** *to acknowledge*, **anvertrauen** *to entrust*, **ausverkaufen** *to sell out* and **vorenthalten** *to withhold*. These behave like separable verbs, but without **ge-** in the past participle: Er **vertraute** es mir **an**. = Er hat es mir **anvertraut**. *He entrusted it to me.* These examples have the separable prefix before the inseparable one. If, on the other hand, the inseparable prefix precedes the separable one, the verb will be an inseparable one throughout, e.g. **beaufsichtigen** *to supervise*, **beabsichtigen** *to intend*, **veranstalten** *to organise*:

Sie **veranstalteten** ein großes Konzert. *They organised a big concert.*

In the rare cases where a double prefix consists of two separable ones, they behave like a single separable prefix, e.g. **voraussagen**, *to predict*, **voraussetzen** *to assume*.

Wir hatten **vorausgesetzt**, daß du um diese Zeit zu Hause bist. *We had assumed that you would be at home at this time.*

Those prefixes which may be either inseparable (and unstressed) or separable (and stressed) are worth careful attention when they combine with the same verb to give two verbs of different meaning, distinguished in the infinitive only by the stress. Here are some examples where both forms of the variable verb are reasonably common (the stressed syllables are in italics):

durchreisen *to traverse,* **durch**reisen *to pass through*:

Er hat ganz England **durchreist**. *He has travelled all over England.*

Er **reiste** ohne Schwierigkeit **durch**. *He travelled through without difficulty.*

übertreten *to violate,* **über**treten *to overflow*:

Sie haben die Vorschrift **übertreten**. *You have broken the regulation.*

Der Fluß **trat über**. *The river overflowed.*

umziehen *to surround,* **um**ziehen *to move house*:

Der Himmel ist mit Wolken **umzogen**. *The sky is overcast* (i.e. *covered in clouds*).

Wir sind vor zwei Wochen **umgezogen**. *We moved house a fortnight ago.*

As will be explained in Chapter 23, verbs in subordinate clauses occupy the final position. When this happens to a separable verb, the prefix remains attached to the verb as in the infinitive or past participle:

Ich weiß nicht, ob er zurückkommt. *I don't know if he's coming back.*

Es schlug zehn Uhr, als er abfuhr. *It was striking ten when he drove off.*

While each new inseparable verb must be studied as one comes across it, it is helpful to note the following aspects and meanings which indicate their force:

be-

1 makes intransitive verbs transitive: **bezahlen** *to pay,* **beantworten** *to answer*;
2 turns an adjective or a noun into a verb meaning 'to cover with', 'supply': **beleuchten** *to illuminate,* **bevölkern** *to populate*.

ent-

1 denotes origin, change, development: **entstehen** *to arise,* **entwikkeln** *to develop,* **entwerfen** *to draft, sketch*;

2 forms opposites: **entdecken** *to discover,* **entfalten** *to unfold;*
3 denotes separation or deprivation: **entnehmen** *to take from,* **entreißen** *to snatch from,* **entziehen** *to deprive of;*
4 with some verbs of motion has the force of 'to escape': **entfliehen** *to run away,* **entkommen** *to escape;*
5 Through assimilation, **ent-** appears as **emp-** in **empfangen** *to receive,* **empfehlen** *to recommend,* **empfinden** *to feel.*

er-
1 denotes achievement: **erreichen** *to attain,* **erfinden** *to invent;*
2 has the force of 'to death': **ermorden** *to murder,* **erschlagen** *to slay.*

miß-
1 forms opposites: **mißverstehen** *to misunderstand,* **mißachten** *to despise;*
2 denotes something done incorrectly or badly: **mißhandeln** *to illtreat,* **mißlingen** *to fail.*

ver-
1 can intensify the meaning: **verlassen** *to abandon,* **verändern** *to alter;*
2 adds the sense of 'away': **vertreiben** *to drive away,* **verraten** to betray;
3 denotes making a mistake: **verwechseln** *to mistake for,* **verpassen** *to miss;*
4 denotes a way of spending time: **verbringen** *to pass time,* **verplaudern** *to chatter away;*
5 adds a negative or unfavourable sense: **verkennen** *to misjudge,* **verlernen** *to unlearn;*
6 forms the opposite of the root verb: **verachten** *to despise,* **verkaufen** *to sell;*
7 forms factitive verbs from adjectives, i.e. with the sense 'to make' + adjective: **verbessern** *to improve,* i.e. make better, **vereinfachen** *to simplify.*

zer- denotes 'apart', 'to pieces': **zerbrechen** *to smash,* **zerreißen** *to tear up.*

The compound verbs considered in this chapter obviously enable one to greatly extend one's vocabulary with little effort as regards the quantity of new material to be assimilated, and if the separable verbs are a little trickier to handle than most, this is compensated for by the fact that the inseparable verbs are simpler than most. We turn next to a small group of absolutely invaluable verbs which well repay study, the modal auxiliaries.

16 Modal Auxiliaries

The verbs **dürfen** *to be allowed to*, **können** *to be able to*, **mögen** *to like to*, **müssen** *to have to*, **sollen** *to ought to* and **wollen** *to want to* are known as modal auxiliaries because they are mainly used in conjunction with other verbs whose significance they modify, expressing respectively permission, ability, inclination, necessity, obligation and volition to perform the action of the associated verb. This associated verb normally occupies the final position in the clause, and is always in the infinitive without any **zu**, for example:

Wir können das Auto nicht finden. *We can't find the car.*

The present tense of modal verbs is irregular: note the absence of a third person singular ending, and the change of vowel in the plural, except for **sollen**:

dürfen	**mögen**	**sollen**
ich darf	ich mag	ich soll
du darfst	du magst	du sollst
er ⎫	er ⎫	er ⎫
sie ⎬ darf	sie ⎬ mag	sie ⎬ soll
es ⎭	es ⎭	es ⎭
wir dürfen	wir mögen	wir sollen
ihr dürft	ihr mögt	ihr sollt
Sie dürfen	Sie mögen	Sie sollen
sie dürfen	sie mögen	sie sollen
können	**müssen**	**wollen**
ich kann	ich muß	ich will
du kannst	du mußt	du willst
er ⎫	er ⎫	er ⎫
sie ⎬ kann	sie ⎬ muß	sie ⎬ will
es ⎭	es ⎭	es ⎭
wir können	wir müssen	wir wollen
ihr könnt	ihr müßt	ihr wollt
Sie können	Sie müssen	Sie wollen
sie können	sie müssen	sie wollen

Although the endings in the simple past are regular, note that the four modal verbs which have an umlaut in the infinitive (**dürfen, können, mögen, müssen**) drop it in the simple past, which is therefore **durfte, konnte, mochte, mußte, sollte** and **wollte.** These irregularities are very slight compared with their equivalents in English, where there is no real infinitive for *may, can, should,* etc., and *must* has not even got a past tense!

Modal verbs are true auxiliaries which cannot stand on their own except when an unspoken verb is "understood", as in **Darf ich?** *May I?*, referring to taking a chair, for example. They do not report action but rather feeling, attitude and disposition, which may overlap to some extent, so that the dividing line between 'You may' and 'You can' is not so clear as that between 'You rise' and 'You fall'.

In the perfect and pluperfect tenses the modal verbs have a regular past participle form **gekonnt, gewollt,** etc., but this is used only on the very rare occasions when the modal verb is on its own: Ich hab' es einfach nicht gekonnt. *I simply couldn't, wasn't able to.* Er hat nicht gewollt. *He was unwilling to.* Normally in their auxiliary function they use the infinitive form for the past participle:

Ich hab' es nicht machen können. *I wasn't able to do it.*

Sie hatte es immer kaufen wollen. *She had always wanted to buy it.*

Ich habe zu Fuß kommen müssen. *I have had to come on foot.*

In the future and conditional tenses, the modal verbs similarly form a sentence with two infinitives at the end:

Wir werden uns beeilen müssen. *We shall have to hurry.*

Ich werde nicht kommen können. *I shall not be able to come.*

Er würde sofort gehen wollen. *He would want to go at once.*

Although the use of modal verbs is quite consistent and logical, English learners are particularly prone to confuse German with English usage in certain cases; for example, it is easy to forget that **ich will** does not mean *I will* but *I want to,* and the correct choice between **müssen** and **dürfen** can elude the unwary. **Ich muß nicht** is *I don't have to* rather than *I must not,* which is more often **Ich darf nicht,** e.g. Ich darf keinen Alkohol trinken. *I mustn't drink alcohol.* Sie dürfen ihn nicht stören. *You mustn't disturb him.* but Das müssen Sie aber nicht. *You don't have to do that.*

There are many expressions in which verbs are omitted or 'understood' after modals, particularly verbs of motion, e.g. Ich will nach München. *I want to go to Munich.* Ich sollte zu meiner Tante. *I was to go to my aunt's.*

Although the subjunctive will be introduced in the next chapter, there are several past subjunctive forms of modal verbs which are so frequently met with as to justify slightly premature introduction here, the more so since in usage they are not so much true subjunctives as shortened conditional forms. Thus **ich möchte** *I should like to* is by far the commonest form of the verb **mögen**, and **ich könnte** *I could, I should be able to*, together with **ich sollte** *I should, I ought to*, are two of the commonest modal forms. Examples:

> Ich **möchte** die Schweiz besuchen.   *I should like to visit Switzerland.*
>
> **Könnten** Sie mir das Geld zurückgeben?   *Could you give me the money back?*
>
> Er **sollte** schon hier sein.   *He should be here already.*
>
> **Möchten** Sie Tee oder Kaffee?   *Would you like tea or coffee?*
>
> Ich **könnte** das Buch heute abend lesen.   *I could read the book this evening.*
>
> Man **sollte** immer geduldig sein.   *One should always be patient.*
>
> Das **dürfte** so sein.   *That may well be so.*
>
> Ich wollt', ich **könnt'** es.   *I wish I could do it.*
>
> Sie ist hübsch, nur **müßte** sie schlanker sein.   *She's pretty, only she ought to be slimmer.*

Note the difference in meaning between the following pairs of sentences:

> Er kann es getan haben.   *He may have done it.*
> Er hat es tun können.   *He has been able to do it.*
>
> Er muß es getan haben.   *He must have done it.*
> Er hat es tun müssen.   *He has had to do it.*
>
> Er soll es getan haben.   *He is said to have done it.*
> Er hat es tun sollen.   *He was supposed to do it.*
>
> Er will es getan haben.   *He claims to have done it.*
> Er hat es tun wollen.   *He meant to have done it.*
>
> Er mag es getan haben.   *He may have done it.*
> Er hat es nicht tun mögen.   *He didn't like to do it.*

Various uses of the individual modals:

> **dürfen**   *to be allowed to; may*
> Hier darf man nicht rauchen.   *Smoking is not allowed here.*
> wenn ich bitten darf   *if you please*
> Was darf es sein, bitte?   *What can I get you?*
> Das darfst du nicht.   *You mustn't do that.*
> Dürfte ich Sie bitten, mich anzurufen?   *Might I ask you to give me a ring?*

können *to be able to; know how to; be in a position to*
Ich kann nicht anders. *I cannot do otherwise.*
Er kann gut Deutsch. *He speaks good German.*
Ich kann mich irren. *I may be wrong.*
Sie kann auf Urlaub sein. *She may be on holiday.*
Wir konnten keinen Ausweg finden. *We couldn't find any way out.*

mögen *to like to; wish to; may*
Ich mag diesen Wein nicht. *I don't like this wine.*
Wer mag das sein? *Who can that be?*
Er mochte sieben Jahre alt sein. *He was perhaps seven years old.*
Meinetwegen mag sie hier bleiben. *So far as I'm concerned she can stay here.*
Möchtest du lieber zu Hause bleiben? *Would you rather stay at home?*

müssen *to have to; be obliged to; must*
Ich muß jetzt nach Hause. *I must go home now.*
Italien muß ein sehr schönes Land sein. *Italy must be a very beautiful country.*
Wir mußten bezahlen, was er wollte. *We had to pay what he wanted.*
Er hat schwer arbeiten müssen. *He's had to work hard.*
Die Straßen sind naß: es muß geregnet haben. *The streets are wet: it must have rained.*

sollen *to be supposed to; said to; ought*
Was soll ich in London tun? *What am I to do in London?*
Sie wußte nicht, was sie tun sollte. *She didn't know what to do.*
Eine neue Universität soll gebaut werden. *A new university is to be built.*
Er soll sehr reich sein. *He is said to be very rich.*
Du solltest dich nicht so benehmen. *You shouldn't behave like that.*

wollen *to want to; intend; mean*
Er will jetzt schlafen. *He wants to sleep now.*
Sie wollten gestern einen Spaziergang machen. *They wanted to go for a walk yesterday.*
Sie wollten etwas sagen? *You were wanting to say something?*
Sie hat ihn gestern sehen wollen. *She wanted to see him yesterday.*
Was will er damit sagen? *What does he mean by that?*

lassen, although not strictly a modal auxiliary, shares features with them, e.g. governing an infinitive with **zu**, denoting 'having something done' or 'something can easily be done':

Er lässt sich die Haare schneiden.   *He is having his hair cut.*

Das Wort lässt sich nicht übersetzen.   *The word cannot be translated.*

Sie müssen einen Anzug machen lassen.   *You must have a suit made.*

At the beginning of this chapter modal auxiliaries were said to be those verbs which modify the meaning of the verbs they serve. Some grammarians prefer to call them auxiliaries of mood, stressing the point that they refer to an attitude towards the action represented by the verb they serve rather than to any action on their own account. The **indicative** mood is used to express factual occurrences – all the tenses we have called 'basic' are indicative in this sense. The **imperative** mood does not represent factual occurrences but instructions and commands ('Do this!' and 'Go away!' are in the imperative mood). The **subjunctive** mood is used to express supposition, doubt and unreality in contrast to the certainty and factual reality of the indicative. This subjunctive mood survives in English in a limited number of more or less fossilised expressions such as: "God save the Queen!" (which could also be described as a third person imperative), "If I were you . . .", "If that be so . . .", "Far be it from me . . ." The subjunctive mood in German, however, is, perhaps regrettably, less defunct than in English, and in the next chapter we shall consider the unavoidable uses of the subjunctive in German, together with the much simpler imperative mood.

17 The Subjunctive and Imperative

All the tenses encountered so far have been in the indicative mood, but for each of them there is an equivalent (fortunately much less frequently encountered) in the subjunctive mood. The commonest forms are the present and simple past of **haben** and **sein** and the simple past of the modal verbs and **werden**, and these, together with the present and simple past of a weak verb (**machen**) are as follows:

PRESENT SUBJUNCTIVE

haben	**sein**	**machen**
ich habe	ich sei	ich mache
du habest	du sei(e)st	du machest
er ⎫ sie ⎬ habe es ⎭	er ⎫ sie ⎬ sei es ⎭	er ⎫ sie ⎬ mache es ⎭
wir haben	wir seien	wir machen
ihr habet	ihr seiet	ihr machet
Sie haben	Sie seien	Sie machen
sie haben	sie seien	sie machen

SIMPLE PAST SUBJUNCTIVE

haben	**sein**	**machen**
ich hätte	ich wäre	ich machte
du hättest	du wär(e)st	du machtest
er ⎫ sie ⎬ hätte es ⎭	er ⎫ sie ⎬ wäre es ⎭	er ⎫ sie ⎬ machte es ⎭
wir hätten	wir wären	wir machten
ihr hättet	ihr wär(e)t	ihr machtet
Sie hätten	Sie wären	Sie machten
sie hätten	sie wären	sie machten

dürfen	**können**	**mögen**	**müssen**
ich dürfte	ich könnte	ich möchte	ich müßte
du dürftest	du könntest	du möchtest	du müßtest
er ⎫	er ⎫	er ⎫	er ⎫
sie ⎬ dürfte	sie ⎬ könnte	sie ⎬ möchte	sie ⎬ müßte
es ⎭	es ⎭	es ⎭	es ⎭
wir dürften	wir könnten	wir möchten	wir müßten
ihr dürftet	ihr könntet	ihr möchtet	ihr müßtet
Sie dürften	Sie könnten	Sie möchten	Sie müßten
sie dürften	sie könnten	sie möchten	sie müßten

sollen	**wollen**	**werden**
ich sollte	ich wollte	ich würde
du solltest	du wolltest	du würdest
er ⎫	er ⎫	er ⎫
sie ⎬ sollte	sie ⎬ wollte	sie ⎬ würde
es ⎭	es ⎭	es ⎭
wir sollten	wir wollten	wir würden
ihr solltet	ihr wolltet	ihr würdet
Sie sollten	Sie wollten	Sie würden
sie sollten	sie wollten	sie würden

These particular tenses are given in full because they are the commonest subjunctives. The present subjunctive of modals is less frequently met (**ich könne, ich dürfe, ich möge, ich müsse, ich solle, ich wolle**) but in general subjunctive tenses are formed quite regularly. Note the persistent -**e** of the endings; that the imperfect subjunctive of all regular weak verbs is the same as the imperfect indicative; and that strong verbs with **a, o** or **u** in the stem of the simple past modify that vowel in the simple past of the subjunctive; thus **sprach** gives **spräche**, **flog** gives **flöge** (cf. **könnte, möchte**) and **fuhr** gives **führe** (cf. **würde**). The compound tenses are formed by adding the past participle or the infinitive, or both, to the auxiliary, precisely as in the indicative. Thus the perfect subjunctive is **er habe gesprochen, er sei gekommen**, the pluperfect subjunctive **er hätte gewartet, er wäre gegangen**, the future subjunctive **er werde erwartet**, the conditional perfect subjunctive **er würde gehabt haben** and so on.

The commonest single form of the subjunctive in German is the simple past subjunctive of **werden**, which is used as an auxiliary to form the conditional tense **ich würde** +infinitive and so on. Apart from this, the subjunctive is most frequently met in the subordinate clauses of indirect or reported speech:

Direct speech:

Sie sagt: "Das Baby hat mein Buch zerrissen." *She says "The baby has torn up my book."*

Er sagte: "Ich werde ihm schreiben." *He said "I shall write to him."*

Indirect speech:

Sie sagte, das Baby habe ihr Buch zerrissen. *She said the baby had torn up her book.*

Er sagte, er werde ihm schreiben. *He said he will write to him.*

The tense of the subjunctive in indirect speech should be the same as that of the original direct speech, provided that the subjunctive and indicative forms are different. Weak verbs have the same form in the simple past indicative and subjunctive, the present subjunctive should be used in indirect speech with them:

"Peter spielt mit Karl." *"Peter is playing with Karl."*

Er sagte, Peter spiele mit Karl. *He said Peter was playing with Karl.*

The subjunctive sometimes occurs in main clauses expressing a wish or instruction; these are usually set expressions:

Es lebe die Königin! *Long live the Queen!*

Dem sei, wie es wolle. *Be that as it may.*

Gott sei Dank! *Thank Heavens!*

Gott behüte! *God forbid!*

Man nehme einen Liter Milch, 4 Eier, . . . *Take one litre of milk, 4 eggs, . . .*

The subjunctive is also used in certain conditional clause sequences, as follows:

(a) If the condition is an improbable one (signified by *would* in English), then the 'if' clause will be in the imperfect subjunctive and the main clause in the conditional or in the imperfect subjunctive:

Wenn ich nur Zeit **hätte**, **würde** ich viel lieber mit dem Zug **fahren**. *If only I had time, I should much rather travel by train.*

Wenn ich mit Frau Weber **sprechen wollte**, **könnte** ich sie **anrufen**. *If I wanted to speak to Frau Weber, I could ring her up.*

(*b*)   If the condition is an impossible one (signified by *would have* in English), then the 'if' clause will be in the pluperfect subjunctive, and the main clause in the pluperfect subjunctive or in the conditional perfect:

> Wenn wir letztes Jahr **gekommen wären, hätten** wir es **gesehen**. OR Wenn wir letztes Jahr **gekommen wären, würden** wir es **gesehen haben**. *If we had come last year we would have seen it.*

(c)   Note that if the condition is an open one (identifiable by containing no *would* or *would have*), then both verbs will be in the indicative: Wenn wir jetzt **losfahren, werden** wir um acht Uhr in Köln **sein**. *If we set off now, we shall be in Cologne at eight o'clock.*

The subjunctive is also found in expressions of wishing, believing, intending, doubting, commanding, advising, requesting and urging, for example:

> Ich hätte gern ein neues Auto.   *I should like to have a new car.*
> Er glaubte, es sei seine Tochter.   *He believed it was his daughter.*
> Ich schrieb alles auf, damit er nicht vergäße.   *I wrote it all down so that he wouldn't forget.*
> Er zweifelte, ob eine andere Lösung möglich wäre.   *He doubted whether any other solution was possible.*

These and similar usages are mentioned here chiefly that the student may be able to recognise them; they can usually be avoided and are rarely necessary – the tendency in the German language today is to use the subjunctive less and less. Its use in reported speech, however, is unavoidable and should be mastered.

The most important thing to be remembered is that the subjunctive expresses the uncertain, the hypothetical and the supposed, whereas the indicative expresses certainty, fact and definite knowledge. Examples which clarify the difference are:

> Er fragte mich, ob ich krank **bin**.   *He asked me if I were ill.*
> Ich fragte ihn, ob er krank **sei**.   *I asked him if he were ill.*
> Ich möchte wissen, ob er **kommt**.   *I wonder if he's coming.*
> Ich fragte mich, ob er **käme**.   *I wondered if he were coming.*

In short, the forms of the subjunctive are on the whole very regular, and its uses are mainly in conditional clauses, indirect speech, a number of exclamatory wishes and some clauses introduced by **damit** (*in order that*) or **als ob** (*as if*). Some may regard its use as an outdated pedantry, while to others it is the acme of elegance, but it is certainly on the periphery rather than at the centre of German grammar.

It was mentioned at the end of the last chapter that in addition to the indicative and subjunctive there is an imperative mood. This is fairly straightforward in German. The imperative mood is referred to in many grammars as the command form; the learner may feel that he is so unlikely to be in a position of issuing commands to Germans that this may safely be ignored, but in fact the form includes most requests: "*Please accept this gift!*" is technically an imperative! In German these forms are made, for **wir** and the polite **Sie**, simply by reversing the verb and pronoun:

> Gehen wir nach Hause! *Let's go home!*
> Kommen Sie mit mir! *Come with me!*
> Bitte, setzen Sie sich! *Please sit down.*

For the familiar **du** and **ihr** forms the pronoun is omitted; in the case of **ihr** one simply has, for example, Kinder, bringt eure Hefte her! *Children, bring your exercise books here!*, and in the case of **du**, the imperative is formed for most verbs by adding -e to the verb stem, for example:

> Fliege, mein Gesang, zur Geliebten! *Fly, my song, to the beloved!*,

though in colloquial speech, which is where most **du** imperatives occur, the final -e is omitted:

> Mutti, bring' mir meine Schuhe! *Mummy, bring me my shoes!*
> Lauf' schnell zum Postamt! *Run quickly to the post office!*

Strong verbs which change **e** to **i** or **ie** in the present tense merely drop the -st of the **du** form to make the imperative, for example:

> Nimm dein Buch zu Vati! *Take your book to Daddy!*
> Sieh den schönen Vogel dort! *Look at the lovely bird there!*
> Gib mir die Hand! *Give me your hand!*

This completes our examination of verbs themselves, and this section on the verb and its associates will continue in the next chapter with a consideration of adverbs.

18   Adverbs

Adverbs are words which indicate how, when, where or to what extent the verb operates, e.g. Er fuhr **schnell** *He drove fast*, Er ist **gestern** angekommen *He arrived yesterday*, Wir sind **hierher** geflogen *We flew here*, Das stimmt **ungefähr** *That's about right*. These are called adverbs of manner, time, place and degree respectively, and in German they are indeclinable. Almost all adjectives may be used as adverbs, in which case, of course, they will be in the invariable predicative form without any ending, e.g. Sie singt **schön** *She sings beautifully*.

While most adverbs are also adjectives, there are many common words which are always and only adverbs, e.g. **außerdem** *besides*, **bald** *soon*, **dort** *there*, **gestern** *yesterday*, **heute** *today*, **hier** *here*, **jetzt** *now*, **nie** *never*, **nur** *only*, **oben** *up above, upstairs*.

If two or more adverbs or adverbial phrases occur in a sentence, they normally come in the following order: 1 **time**, 2 **manner**, 3 **place**, thus:

> Ich fahre **morgen mit dem Zug nach Bonn**.   *I am going to Bonn by train tomorrow.*
>
> Wir sollen **direkt zum Büro** fahren.   *We are to go straight to the office.*
>
> Er wird mich **früh mit dem Wagen zum Flughafen** bringen.   *He'll take me to the airport early by car.*

Though shorter items may on occasion take priority:

> Ich fühle mich **hier ganz zu Hause**.   *I feel quite at home here.*

If two adverbs of the same sort occur in a sentence, the more general precedes the more specific:

> Wir werden uns **heute um zwei Uhr** treffen.   *We shall meet today at two o'clock.*
>
> Er sitzt **im Garten auf der Bank**.   *He is sitting on the bench in the garden.*

The comparative form of adverbs is formed like that of adjectives by adding **-er**:

> Hans fährt **schneller** als sein Vater.   *Hans drives faster than his father.*

Ich werde **langsamer** sprechen. *I shall speak more slowly.*

The superlative form of adverbs, however, is formed with **am** before the superlative with the ending -**en**, for example:

Heinz fährt **am schnellsten**. *Heinz drives the fastest.*

Die älteste Tochter sang **am schönsten**. *The eldest daughter sang the most beautifully.*

There are a few adverbs with irregular comparative and superlative forms:

bald	*soon*	eher	am ehesten
		früher	am frühsten
gern	*gladly*	lieber	am liebsten
gut	*well*	besser	am besten
hoch	*highly*	höher	am höchsten
nah	*closely*	näher	am nächsten
oft	*often*	öfter	am öftesten
viel	*much*	mehr	am meisten

It should be noted that some words in English may in different contexts be an adverb, preposition or conjunction, e.g. before, after: *I have seen him before* (adverb); *I saw him before dawn* (preposition); *I saw him before he left* (conjunction). In German, the different functions are represented by different words: the adverbs are **vorher**, **nachher**, the prepositions **vor**, **nach**, and the conjunctions **bevor**, **nachdem**.

In the adverbs **vorher**, **nachher**, we have the component -**her**, which, together with its twin -**hin**, forms a whole range of pairs of adverbs. **Hin** is used to indicate direction away from the speaker and **her** to indicate direction towards the speaker, as the following examples may demonstrate:

Ich gehe **hinauf**. *I am going up, i.e. away from here.*

Kommen Sie **herauf**! *Come up, i.e. towards here.*

Wohin gehen Sie? *Where are you going?*

Woher kommen Sie? *Where do you come from?*

Similarly **dorthin** and **dahin** both mean *thither*, while **dorther** and **daher** both mean *thence*.

Although the principal function of adverbs, as their name implies, is to modify verbs, they may also modify adjectives:

Das ist **höchst interessant**. *That is most interesting.*

Sie war **recht enttäuscht**. *She was quite disappointed.*

or other adverbs, e.g.

Er fährt **sehr schnell**. *He drives very fast.*

Er spielt **ziemlich gut**. *He plays fairly well.*

or even conjunctions:

> Es steht **unmittelbar vor** der Tür. *It stands immediately in front of the door.*
>
> Er ging **gleich nach** dem Frühstück. *He went straight after breakfast.*

In addition to the basic form of a predicative adjective, there are a number of suffixes which are used to form adverbs (rather like the commonest English adverbial suffix -*ly*). They include:

1 -**lich**, as in **bekanntlich** *as is well known*, **bitterlich** *bitterly*, **freilich** *indeed*, **kürzlich** *recently*, **lediglich** *solely*, **schwerlich** *hardly*, **sicherlich** *certainly*, **treulich** *faithfully*;

2 -**s**, as in **abends** *in the evening*, **allerdings**, *certainly*, **anders** *otherwise*, **anfangs** *in the beginning*, **besonders** *especially*, **links** *on the left*, **rechts** *on the right*, **nachts** *at night*;

3 **weise**, as in **ausnahmsweise** *exceptionally*, **beispielsweise** *by way of example*, **beziehungsweise** *respectively*, **glücklicherweise** *fortunately*, **merkwürdigerweise** *strange to say*, **normalerweise** *in the normal course of events*, **schrittweise** *step by step*, **teilweise** *partly*.

This last group tends to convey the speaker's or writer's view of the matter:

> Sie war **merkwürdig müde**. *She was strangely tired.*
>
> Sie war **merkwürdigerweise müde**. *Strange to say, she was tired.*

There are many categories of adverb, which is another way of saying that the adverb is really the rag-bag of the parts of speech; if one is in any doubt as to what part of speech a given word is, it usually turns out to be an adverb.

Thus, firstly, it follows that the separable prefixes are mostly adverbs, with meanings as follows: **ab** *down, away*, **auf** *up*, **fort, los** and **weg** *away*, **nieder** *down*, **weiter** *further, on*, **wieder** *again*, **zurück** *back*, **zusammen** *together*, though some are prepositions only, e.g. **über** and **unter**, which have corresponding adverbial forms **oben** and **unten**. Secondly, many interrogative words are adverbs – **wann?** *when?*, **warum?** *why?*, **weshalb?** *on account of what?*, **wie?** *how?*, **wo?** *where?* and its many compounds **woher?**, **wohin?**, **wodurch?**, **womit?**, **woran?**, **worauf?**, **worin?**, **worüber?**, **worum?**, **wovon?** and **wozu?**, though some are pronouns only, e.g. **wer?** and **was?** Thirdly, a number of very common words are, though this is perhaps not immediately apparent, adverbs – of time: **damals** *then*, **sofort** and **sogleich** *immediately*, **stets** and **immer** *always*; – of place: **außen** *outside*, **vorne** *in front*; – of degree: **fast** *almost*, **genug** *enough*; or finally (not to use the term rag-bag again) miscellaneous: **ja, nein, nicht, noch, nun** and one which merits a section on its own: **gern**.

The basic meaning of **gern** is *gladly, willingly*:

Ich würde **gern** zehn Mark geben. *I would gladly/willingly give ten marks.*

The choice between **gern** and its alternative form **gerne** is usually made on grounds of euphony, e.g. if the following word begins with **g**, **gerne** is preferable, and in general **gerne** sounds warmer than **gern**, but it is not a matter of any importance. Most commonly, however, it adds to a verb the sense of *liking* to do that particular action; note the English translation of the following:

Wir essen gern Fisch. *We like eating fish.*

Ich gehe gern in die Oper. *I like going to the opera.*

Die Kinder schwimmen gern. *The children like swimming.*

Er trinkt gern Schnaps. *He likes drinking Schnapps.*

The comparative and superlative forms **lieber** and **am liebsten** (which really belong to a much more old-fashioned word *lieb* which has now largely disappeared) have a similar effect:

Ich habe Düsseldorf **gern**. *I like Düsseldorf.*

Ich habe Stuttgart **lieber** als Düsseldorf. *I like Stuttgart better than Düsseldorf.*

Ich habe München **am liebsten**. *I like Munich best of all.*

Ich gehe **gern** spazieren; ich reite **lieber**; ich schwimme **am liebsten**. *I like walking; I prefer riding; I like swimming best of all.*

Common idiomatic expressions with **gern** include:

Gerne geschehen! *Don't mention it! Glad to help! – in response to thanks.*

Dieses Modell wird gern gekauft. *This model is very popular.*

Er ist überall gern gesehen. *He is welcome everywhere.*

These are the most important features of the use of standard adverbs, but before concluding our treatment of the verb and its associates, we must look at a very peculiar group of adverbs which are non-standard, in that it is very rarely possible to translate them directly at all, their effect being to modify the tone of the utterance in which they are used. These words are called particles.

19 Particles

The importance of particles is well expressed by A. E. Hammer in his excellent and compendious *German Grammar and Usage* (to which this book is immensely indebted throughout), when he writes (p. 145) 'Colloquial German stands or falls by an ample scattering of **denn**, **doch**, **ja**, **mal**, **schon**, **so** etc., without which it sounds bleak and impersonal.' These words are exceedingly difficult to translate, and often supply the sentence with a tone which in English is communicated purely by the intonation and so exists only in the spoken and not in the written language. The student can acquire skill in their use only by noting every occurrence and thus developing his feeling for the language.

These particles – more correctly termed modal particles – have a few parallels in English in the usage of words like *just* and *only* and expressions like *you know* and *you see*, which similarly have uses apparently unrelated to the original literal or surface meaning. The most important ones are **auch**, **denn**, **doch**, **eben**, **eigentlich**, **etwa**, **ja**, **mal**, **nämlich**, **noch**, **nur**, **schon** and **wohl**. At this point we have not given an English translation in brackets. While they have in their basic adverbial use a consistent English equivalent (**auch** = *also*, **ja** = *yes* and so on), it is precisely because as modal particles they do not have a consistent English equivalent that this chapter is necessary.

A helpful paraphrase for 'modal particles' is 'attitude words', because their real function is to add to the message an indication of the speaker's attitude, whether, for example, encouraging, admonitory, incredulous, insistent, protesting, acquiescent, expecting agreement or disagreement as the case may be, and so on.

Thus **auch**, always appearing as a separate word, corresponds to the English *-ever* in such compound words as *whoever*, *whatever* and sometimes *however:*

> Wer es **auch** sein mag, ich kann ihn jetzt nicht sprechen. *Whoever it may be, I can't talk to him now.*
>
> Was **auch** geschieht, du kannst auf mich zählen. *Whatever happens, you can count on me.*

So schön es **auch** ist, es kostet doch allzu viel. *However beautiful it is, it costs far too much.*

It also has the meaning of *even*:

Auch ein Kind kann das begreifen. *Even a child can understand that.*

Ich gehe spazieren, **auch** wenn schlechtes Wetter ist. *I go walking even when the weather is bad.*

Auch in Kriegszeiten war das erlaubt. *That was allowed even in wartime.*

With a negative it can mean *either, neither* or *nor*:

Er darf nicht gehen – du **auch** nicht. *He can't go – nor can you.*

Er wußte nichts davon – ich **auch** nicht. *He knew nothing about it – neither did I.*

Das wird ihm **auch** nichts helfen. *That won't help him either.*

Often it needs no translation, or may be rendered by *really*:

Er scheint intelligent zu sein. Das ist er **auch**. *He seems intelligent. He is too!*

Was hätte es **auch** für einen Sinn gehabt? *What would have been the point of it?*

Er hat es vorausgesagt, und es ist **auch** geschehen. *He predicted it, and it really happened.*

denn inserted in a question implies interest or makes the question less abrupt:

Wieso **denn**? *How so?*

Was ist **denn** los? *Whatever's the matter?*

Wie geht es Ihnen **denn**? *Tell me, how are you?*

It is also used to intensify suggestions, commands, etc.:

also **denn**! *come on then!*

gehen wir **denn**! *let's go then!*

komm herein **denn**! *come on in!*

Often it needs no translation:

Was halten Sie **denn** davon? *What do you think of it?*

Ist es **denn** wirklich wahr? *Is it really true?*

Hast du das **denn** wirklich gern? *Do you really like that?*

denn doch expresses indignation or protest:

Das geht **denn doch** zu weit! *That's going too far!*

Das ist **denn doch** unerhört! *That really is scandalous!*

doch is used to give an affirmative response where a negative one is expected:

Er war nicht zu Hause? **Doch**. *Wasn't he at home? Yes, he was.*

Das kann ich mir nicht leisten. **Doch**! *I can't afford that. Yes, you can.*

It also intensifies an imperative, often adding a pleading tone:

> Regen Sie sich **doch** nicht so auf! *Please don't get so excited!*
> Nehmen Sie **doch** Platz! *Do take a seat!*

It is often used to contradict or correct the previous utterance:

> Es macht **doch** etwas aus. *But it does matter.*
> Er wird **doch** kommen. *Yes he will come.*

and can also add a sense of 'if only':

> Hättest du es mir **doch** gesagt! *If only you had told me!*
> Wenn er **doch** käme! *If only he would come!*

eben usually corresponds to English *just, exactly* or *precisely*:

> Er ist **eben** angekommen. *He has just this moment arrived.*
> Das wollte ich **eben** sagen. *I was just going to say that.*
> Es ist nicht **eben** angenehm. *It's not exactly pleasant.*

Sometimes it need not be translated, or may be rendered by *simply*:

> Er hat es **eben** nicht gewußt. *He simply didn't know it.*
> Man muß das Leben nehmen, wie es **eben** ist. *One must take life as it is.*

Note that **eben** never means *even*, which is **sogar** or **selbst**.

eigentlich is *actually* or *in reality*, or even *tell me*:

> Was ist **eigentlich** mit ihm los? *What is actually the matter with him?*
> Wir wollten **eigentlich** nach Bonn. *We were really intending to go to Bonn.*
> Wo ist **eigentlich** der Korkenzieher? *Tell me where the corkscrew is.*
> Ist er **eigentlich** krank? *Tell me, is he ill?*

It is often a sort of padding particle which removes any brusqueness from a question:

> Wieviel Leute hast du **eigentlich** eingeladen? *How many people did you actually ask?*

etwa, apart from its basic meaning of *approximately*, can imply a certain reluctance or even incredulity towards the interlocutor:

> Wollen Sie **etwa** behaupten . . . ? *Do you mean to tell me . . . ?*
> Sie wollen ihn doch nicht **etwa** verteidigen? *You don't mean to defend him, do you?*

and can also mean *perhaps, by chance*:

> Ist er **etwa** verreist? *Can he be away?*
> Kennen Sie ihn **etwa**? *Do you happen to know him?*

ja may play the part of a very wide range of English equivalents – *indeed, of course, certainly, to be sure, you know, after all, don't you see, why, surely*:

Ich kann es **ja** versuchen . . . *I can try, of course, . . .*

Es ist **ja** schwer, aber . . . *It's certainly difficult, but . . .*

Ja, wenn es so ist, . . . *Well, if that's how it is, . . .*

Ich habe **ja** nicht viel Arbeit. *I've not much work on, as you know.*

Da ist **ja** Tante Irmgard! *Why, there's Aunt Irmgard!*

but most commonly it defies actual translation, imparting rather a tone of reassurance, reinforcement, assertion, etc. as the case may be:

Der Hund beißt **ja** nicht. *The dog doesn't bite.*

Tu das **ja** nicht! *Mind you don't do that!*

Er soll sich **ja** nicht denken, daß . . . *He'd better not think that . . .*

Das ist es **ja** eben! *That's just the point!*

mal (sometimes in full – **einmal**) is more often than not better left untranslated; it lends a pleasant informality of tone. **nicht (ein) mal** is *not even*:

Sie wollte mich **nicht einmal** sehen. *She wouldn't even see me.*

Er kann **nicht mal** das einfachste Problem lösen. *He can't even solve the simplest problem.*

Das ist nun **mal** so. *That's the way it is.*

Sehen Sie **mal** her! *Just look here!*

Ich hab' ihn **mal** gesehen. *I saw him once.*

Hören Sie **mal**! *Just listen!*

Sagen Sie **mal**, wo wohnen Sie jetzt? *Tell me, where are you living now?*

mal sehen! *let's have a look!*

Moment **mal**! *Just wait a moment!*

nämlich, in addition to its primary meaning of *namely, viz.*, is *you see*:

Er ist **nämlich** etwas kurzsichtig. *He's rather shortsighted, you see.*

Ich muß mich beeilen, ich habe **nämlich** noch vieles zu erledigen. *I must rush, I've a lot to attend to yet, you see.*

noch, in addition to its primary meaning of *yet, still, another, even*, indicates an additional action, whether performed or not:

Was möchten Sie sich **noch** ansehen? *What else would you like to see?*

Wolltest du nicht **noch** zur Bank? *Didn't you want to go to the bank as well?*

Ich möchte **noch** schnell einen Anruf machen. *I just want to make a quick call.*

Sonst **noch** etwas? *Anything else?*

nur, in addition to its primary meaning of *only*, may have intensifying force:

> Das macht es **nur** noch schlimmer. *That makes it even worse.*
> Wie kann er **nur** so taktlos sein? *However can he be so tactless?*
> **Nur** nicht böse! *Don't be angry!*
> Was hast du **nur** vor? *What on earth are you up to?*

schon, in addition to its primary meaning of *already*, is used to reassure:

> Vati wird **schon** kommen. *Daddy will come, I'm sure.*

and to indicate acceptance of the interlocutor's view:

> Das stimmt **schon**, aber . . . *That's quite true, but . . .*
> Ja, ich glaube **schon**, aber . . . *Yes, I quite agree, but . . .*

wohl does not usually mean *well* (which is normally **gut**), but *probably* – it expects agreement, rather like *presumably, I suppose*:

> Er ist **wohl** schon hier. *He is probably here already.*
> Du weißt **wohl**, daß er schon weg ist. *I suppose you know he's already left.*
> Er hat **wohl** den Zug verpaßt. *He has presumably missed the train.*

This must suffice for the moment as an introduction to a fascinating and attractive aspect of the German language – **es ist doch nun mal so**! It ends the second part of this book, concerned with the verb and its associates, and in the third part we shall attempt to bring together the disparate bits of information about the noun and the verb for the purpose of building sentences. This will involve consideration of linking words such as prepositions and conjunctions and also the matter of word order.

PART THREE
Putting It Together

20 Prepositions and the Cases They Govern

Prepositions are words which indicate the relationship between a noun or pronoun which they govern and the rest of the utterance. The German for preposition is **das Verhältniswort** (literally *the relationship word*). Thus in the sentence "*I'll come to town with you.*" the prepositions *to* and *with* indicate how the pronouns *I* and *you*, the noun *town* and the verb *come* are connected.

Prepositions in German are grouped according to whether the noun or pronoun they govern must be in the accusative, dative or genitive case or, with a fourth group, sometimes in the accusative and sometimes in the dative. There are dozens of prepositions, particularly among those governing the genitive, which one very rarely encounters, and this chapter will confine its attention to the really common ones in everyday use, which do not number more than thirty.

The prepositions governing the accusative only are **bis, durch, für, gegen, ohne, um**:

bis means *till, until, by* (before a time expression), *as far as* (before a place expression), *or, to* (with numerals):

Also, auf Wiedersehen – **bis nächsten Freitag**! *Goodbye then – till next Friday!*

Kannst du es **bis nächsten Montag** fertig haben? *Can you have it ready by next Monday?*

Wir fahren **bis Frankfurt**. *We're going as far as Frankfurt.*

Ich brauche zwei **bis drei Tage**. *I need two or three days.*

Sie kosten 20 **bis 30 Mark**. *They cost 20 to 30 marks.*

durch means *through, by means of, by the agency of*:

Sie gucken **durch das Schlüsselloch**. *They are peeping through the keyhole.*

Die Stadt wurde **durch ein Erdbeben** zerstört. *The town was destroyed by an earthquake.*

Er erfuhr die Nachricht **durch einen Freund**.   *He learned the news from a friend.*

für means *for* in a wide range of senses, sometimes *as*:

Er arbeitet **für seinen Bruder**.   *He works for his brother.*

Ich verkaufte den Wagen **für 3 000 Mark**.   *I sold the car for 3,000 marks.*

Sie nahm das **für eine Beleidigung**.   *She took that as an insult.*

gegen is *against, in return for, approximately, towards, compared with*:

Er schwimmt **gegen den Strom**.   *He is swimming against the current.*

Sie vertauschte ihren Schmuck **gegen Lebensmittel**.   *She exchanged her jewellery for food.*

Gegen dreißig Autos warteten am Übergang.   *About thirty cars were waiting at the crossing.*

Gegen seinen Onkel ist er arm.   *Compared with his uncle he is poor.*

ohne is *without*; note that after **ohne** the indefinite article or possessive adjective is often omitted:

Ohne Löffel kann ich die Suppe nicht essen.   *I can't eat the soup without a spoon.*

Sabine ist heute **ohne Kinder** gekommen.   *Sabine has come without her children today.*

Ohne mich!   *Count me out!*

um is *around, at* in time expressions, and occurs in a number of idioms involving a sense of deprivation; in its first sense it is often strengthened by **rings** or **herum**:

Das Geschäft ist gleich **um die Ecke**.   *The shop is just around the corner.*

Wir standen **rings um den Tisch**.   *We stood around the table.*

Die Kinder laufen **um den Teich herum**.   *The children are running around the pond.*

Wir essen gewöhnlich **um acht Uhr**.   *We usually eat at eight o'clock.*

Die Aufregung hat mich **um den Schlaf** gebracht.   *The excitement deprived me of my sleep.*

Er ist **um sein ganzes Geld** gekommen.   *He has lost all his money.*

The chief prepositions which always govern the dative are **aus, bei, gegenüber, mit, nach, seit, von, zu**:

aus means *out of* or *from*:

 Sie kam **aus dem Haus**. *She came out of the house.*
 Ich bin **aus München**. *I am from Munich.*
 Er hat es **aus Angst** getan. *He did it out of fear.*
 Sie war **aus guter Familie**. *She was from a good family.*

bei is *near, by, at the house of, with*:

 Es gibt eine Telefonzelle **bei der Kirche**. *There is a telephone kiosk near the church.*
 Er wohnt **bei seiner Tante**. *He lives with his aunt.*
 Ich habe leider kein Geld **bei mir**. *Unfortunately I have no money on me.*
 Wir haben ihn **bei Schillers** getroffen. *We met him at the Schillers.*
 Sie trafen sich nur **bei Nacht**. *They used to meet only by night.*

gegenüber means *opposite* or *with regard to*, and normally follows the word it governs, though on occasion it may precede it:

 Mir gegenüber saß ein älterer Herr. *Opposite me sat an elderly gentleman.*
 Seinem Vater gegenüber würde er das nicht sagen. *He wouldn't say that to his father.*
 Gegenüber diesen Tatsachen war ich machtlos. *Faced with these facts I was powerless.*

mit covers all straightforward meanings of *with* and often renders *by*:

 Ich esse zu Mittag **mit meinen Kollegen**. *I have lunch with my colleagues.*
 Ich fahre jeden Tag **mit dem Zug** zur Arbeit. *I travel to work every day by train.*
 Das habe ich **mit der Post** geschickt. *I sent that by post.*
 Ich werde **mit ihm** sprechen. *I'll have a word with him.*

nach is *after, to* or *according to*:

 Wir werden **nach dem Konzert** essen. *We shall eat after the concert.*
 Bitte, **nach Ihnen**! *After you, please!*
 Ich fliege morgen **nach New York**. *I'm flying to New York tomorrow.*
 Ich wähle nicht **nach dem Preis**, sondern **nach der Qualität**. *I choose according to the quality, not according to the price.*
 Meiner Meinung nach *In my opinion*

seit is *since* or *for* with expressions of time:

 Seit dem Tod meines Vaters wohne ich hier. *I've lived here since my father died.*

Seit Januar arbeitet er nicht mehr. *He hasn't been working since January.*

Ich arbeite hier **seit zwei Jahren**. *I've been working here for two years.*

Ich bin **seit acht Tagen** hier. *I've been here for a week.*

Note the use of the present tense in German in the above examples.

von is *from* or *of* or *by*:

Ich habe einen Brief **von meinem Vater** bekommen. *I've had a letter from my father.*

Ein Mann **von russischer Abstammung** *A man of Russian descent*

Er wurde **von dem Lehrer** gelobt. *He was praised by the teacher.*

Ein Pfund **von diesem Käse** *A pound of this cheese*

Kennst du diesen Roman **von Thomas Mann**? *Do you know this novel by Thomas Mann?*

Sie war **vom ersten** bis zum zehnten April da. *She was there from the first to the tenth of April.*

zu is generally *to* or *at* or *in*:

Ich gehe **zu seiner Mutter**. *I'm going to his mother.*

Er paßte nicht **zu einer solchen Stelle**. *He was not suitable for such a post.*

J. S. Bach wurde **zu Eisenach** geboren. *J. S. Bach was born in Eisenach.*

Er kehrte **zu seiner Arbeit** zurück. *He went back to his work.*

Zu jener Zeit gab es keine Eisenbahn. *At that time there was no railway.*

The chief prepositions governing the genitive are **statt**, **trotz**, **während** and **wegen**:

statt, which also occurs in the form **anstatt**, means *instead of*:

Statt eines Briefes schrieb er nur eine Karte. *Instead of a letter he only wrote a card.*

Anstatt der Tochter kam die Mutter. *The mother came instead of the daughter.*

trotz (which may take the dative on occasion) means *in spite of, despite*:

Trotz des Regens haben wir Fußball gespielt. *We played football in spite of the rain.*

während is *during*:

Wahrend des Krieges war mein Vater in der Schule. *During the war my father was at school.*

wegen is *on account of, because of*:

Wegen des schlechten Wetters bleibe ich zu Hause. *Because of the bad weather I'm staying in.*

The following prepositions take accusative when motion is implied (answering the question *Whither?* or *Where to?*) and dative when location is indicated (*Where?*): **an, auf, hinter, in, neben, über, unter, vor** and **zwischen:**

Ich schreibe **an meinen Bruder.** *I am writing to my brother.*

Das Bild hängt **an der Wand.** *The picture hangs on the wall.*

Ich lege das Buch **auf den Tisch.** *I put the book on the table.*

Das Buch ist **auf dem Tisch.** *The book is on the table.*

Das Baby kriecht **hinter das Sofa.** *The baby crawls behind the sofa.*

Das Dorf liegt **hinter diesem Berg.** *The village lies behind this mountain.*

Ich gehe jetzt **in den Garten.** *I'm going into the garden now.*

Ich wohne **in diesem Haus.** *I live in that house.*

Ich stelle den Bücherschrank **neben die Tür.** *I'll put the bookcase beside the door.*

Da steht sie, **neben der Tür.** *There she is, standing beside the door.*

Sie gehen **über die Brücke.** *They're going across the bridge.*

Über dem Tisch hängt eine Lampe. *Above the table hangs a lamp.*

Das Messer ist **unter den Tisch** gefallen. *The knife has fallen under the table.*

Unter meinem Fenster wächst eine Rose. *A rose grows underneath my window.*

Er trat **vor den General** hin. *He stepped up to the general.*

Er stand **vor dem General.** *He stood before the general.*

Er setzte sich **zwischen die beiden Jungen.** *He sat down between the two boys.*

Sie saß **zwischen ihren Eltern.** *She was sitting between her parents.*

In other contexts, if the notion of rest or movement cannot be even figuratively applied, **auf** and **über** preponderantly take the accusative and the others the dative.

The next chapter will show how some prepositions combine with certain other words, and mention some other features concerning the use of prepositions.

21 The Use of Prepositions

Prepositions and the definite article are frequently combined into a single word as follows: **an, auf, durch, für, in, um** + accusative **das = ans, aufs, durchs, fürs, ins, ums**; less commonly one may meet **hinters, übers, unters** and **vors. an, bei, in, von, zu** + dative **dem = am, beim, im, vom, zum**; again one may come across, though less frequently, **hinterm, überm, unterm, vorm**. The only contracted form with a feminine article is **zu + der**, which becomes **zur**. Most grammar books state that it is correct to use either the contraction or the two-word form, but this is far from being the case. The contracted forms are normally expected unless there is some reason to stress the article, and one really must use them in such expressions as, for example, **im Gegenteil** *on the contrary*, **im allgemeinen** *in general*, **zum Beispiel** *for example* and **im Freien** *in the open air*, where the two-word form could not be called correct.

Another important group of prepositional compounds is formed with the prefix **da-** (corresponding to English *therefore, therewith* and so on); thus we may have **dabei, dadurch, dafür, dagegen, dahinter, damit, danach, daneben, davon, davor, dazu** and **dazwischen**. If the preposition begins with a vowel, an **r** is inserted, giving **daran, darauf, daraus, darin, darüber, darum** and **darunter**. No other prepositions combine with **da**. These compounds with **da** replace preposition + pronoun referring to inanimate objects; the two-word form is retained for persons:

Was hast du **für ihn** gemacht? *What did you do for him*?
Was hast du **dafür** bezahlt? *What did you pay for it*?

Generally speaking, these compounds are not used where a sense of motion must be conveyed, thus **darin** means *in it* but not *into it*, which would be **hinein**, and other words with **hin** and **her** would be used to express motion, e.g. **hindurch** and not **dadurch**, in other contexts. The normal stress on all these compound words is on the second syllable, unless they are being used emphatically, in which case they are stressed on the first syllable.

When the interrogative pronoun, referring to a thing and not a person, is used with the prepositions mentioned in the previous paragraph (with the exceptions of **neben** and **zwischen**), the usual form is **wo** + preposition, instead of preposition + **was;** thus we may have **wobei, wodurch, wofür, wogegen, wohinter, womit, wonach, wovon, wovor** and **wozu.** If the preposition begins with a vowel, an **r** is inserted, giving **woran, worauf, woraus, worin, worüber, worum** and **worunter.** No other prepositions combine with **wo.** An example of its use is as follows:

Mit wem bist du gekommen? *Who did you come with?*
Womit schreibst du? *What are you writing with?*

When compounded with **wo, durch, nach, von** and **zu** do not generally express motion, for which purpose one would resort to **durch was, woher** and **wohin:**

Wodurch ist er so reich geworden? *How did he become so rich?*
Wonach fragt sie? *What is she asking about?*
Wovon lebt er? *What does he live on?*
Wozu kann man das brauchen? *What can one use that for?*
BUT
Wohin reisen Sie? (not **wonach**) *Where are you travelling to?*
Woher kommen Sie? (not **wovon**) *Where do you come from?*

In German, as in English, certain verbs are always followed by a particular preposition, but unfortunately choosing the correct one is not simply a matter of selecting the equivalent of the English preposition. The whole business is a minefield, and the best we can do is to list here some of the commonest collocations:

an

arbeiten an (+dat.) *to work at, on*
(sich) erinnern an (+acc.) *to remind (remember)*
erkennen an (+dat.) *to recognise by*
(sich) gewöhnen an (+acc.) *to accustom*
glauben an (+acc.) *to believe in*

leiden an (+dat.) *to suffer from*
sterben an (+dat.) *to die of*
stoßen an (+acc.) *to knock against*
teilnehmen an (+dat.) *to take part in*
zweifeln an (+dat.) *to doubt*

auf

(sich) beschränken auf (+acc.) *to restrict*
bestehen auf (+dat.) *to insist on*
sich freuen auf (+acc.) *to look forward to*

rechnen auf (+acc.) *to count on*
sich verlassen auf (+acc.) *to rely on*
verzichten auf (+acc.) *to forgo, renounce*

hoffen auf (+ acc.) *to hope
for*

weisen auf (+ acc.) *to point to,
at*

aus

bestehen aus *to consist of*
entstehen aus *to arise from*

schließen aus *to infer from*
stammen aus *to originate
from (place); to date back to
(time)*

bei

arbeiten bei *to work with
(a firm), for (a person)*
dienen bei *to serve with
(the Forces)*

nehmen bei *to take by
(e.g. the hand)*
packen bei *to seize by
(e.g. the hair)*

nach

fragen nach *to enquire about*
riechen nach *to smell of*

schmecken nach *to taste of*
urteilen nach *to judge by*

über

klagen über *to complain of,
about*
lachen über *to laugh at,
about*
nachdenken über *to reflect
on*

sprechen über *to speak about*

verfügen über *to have at
one's disposal*
weinen über *to cry about*

um

bitten um *to ask for, beg for*
kämpfen um *to fight for*

streiten um *to quarrel about*
trauern um *to mourn for*

von

abhängen von *to depend on*
handeln von *to deal with,
be about*
leben von *to live on*

sprechen von *to speak of*
träumen von *to dream of*

überzeugen von *to convince of*

vor

erröten vor *to blush for
e.g. shame*
fliehen vor *to flee from*
retten vor *to rescue from*

schützen vor *to protect from*

warnen vor *to warn of, against*
zittern vor *to tremble with
(e.g. fear)*

zu

dienen zu *to serve, be useful for*	taugen zu *to be fit for, good for*
gratulieren zu *to congratulate on*	werden zu *to become*

In addition to these and many other less common constructions in which a particular preposition is associated with a certain verb, there are innumerable expressions in which the preposition normal with a given noun, adjective or whatever, does not correspond to English usage. Here is a selection of the most useful instances:

an + acc.
Jetzt komme ich an die Reihe.   *It's my turn now.*
Er ist an solche Krisen gewohnt.   *He's used to such crises.*
Mein Bericht an die Direktoren   *My report to the directors*

an + dat.
Jetzt bist du an der Reihe.   *It's your turn now.*
Am folgenden Tag . . .   *The next day . . .*
An deiner Stelle würde ich . . .   *If I were you, I should . . .*

auf + acc.
auf diese Weise   *in this way*
auf jeden Fall   *in any case*
Wir sind stolz auf dich!   *We are proud of you!*

auf + dat.
auf dem Bahnhof   *at the station*
auf der Straße   *in the street*
auf dem Lande   *in the country*

aus
Wir wissen es aus Erfahrung.   *We know from experience.*
aus Baumwolle   *made of cotton*
aus Gewohnheit   *from habit*

bei
bei meiner Tante   *at my aunt's*
bei gutem Wetter   *in good weather*
bei meiner Ankunft   *on my arrival*
bei dieser Gelegenheit   *on this occasion*
bei einem Glas Wein   *over a glass of wine*

für
Jahr für Jahr   *year after year*
schädlich für   *detrimental to*

gegen
gegen 4 Uhr   *about four o'clock*
gegen Ende des Jahres   *towards the end of the year*
empfindlich gegen   *sensitive to*

in + acc.
in Ordnung bringen   *to tidy*
Ich schnitt mich in die Hand.   *I cut my hand.*
verliebt in   *in love with*

in + dat.
in der Nacht   *at night*
im Augenblick   *at the moment*
im Gegensatz zu   *in contrast to*

mit
mit Absicht   *intentionally, on purpose*
mit lauter Stimme   *in a loud voice*
mit dem Kopf nicken   *to nod one's head*

nach
nach Hause   *homewards*
meiner Meinung nach   *in my opinion*
allem Anschein nach   *to all appearances*
begierig nach   *eager for*

über + acc.
ein Bericht über   *a report on*
froh/traurig über   *glad/sad about*
Wir fahren über Hamburg.   *We are travelling via Hamburg.*
enttäuscht über   *disappointed in*

unter + dat.
unter uns   *amongst/between ourselves*
unter dieser Bedingung   *on this condition*
unter diesen Umständen   *in these circumstances*

zu
zu Hause   *at home*
zu Fuß   *on foot*
zu Ostern, Weihnachten   *at Easter, Christmas*

This outline of typical prepositional constructions shows how the simplest utterances develop into more complex structures. The following chapter will show how sentences and clauses are linked together.

22 Conjunctions

Conjunctions are indeclinable words used to link words, clauses and sentences together. The commonest conjunction *and*, for example, may link words: *My cat is black and white.*, clauses: *He knocked at the door and ran away.*, or sentences: *The war ended, and a new age began.* The most important thing to remember about German conjunctions is that some of them have an effect upon the word order of the clause they introduce. Those which do have such an effect (and they are the majority) are called subordinating conjunctions, and those which leave the word order unaffected are called co-ordinating conjunctions.

The co-ordinating conjunctions are so called because the clauses they connect are co-ordinate clauses, i.e. equal in importance and potential independence: each of them could be a main clause forming a sentence on its own. The co-ordinating conjunctions in normal use are **aber** *but*, **denn** *for*, **oder** *or*, **und** *and* and **sondern**, *but* (in a special sense – see below):

Er ist fleißig **aber** dumm. *He is hard-working but stupid.*

Ich wartete eine Stunde, **aber** das Café blieb leer. *I waited an hour, but the café remained empty.*

Sie kommt heute nicht, **denn** sie hat Besuch. *She's not coming today, for she has visitors.*

Ich konnte nicht gehen, **denn** ich war krank. *I couldn't go, as I was ill.*

Möchten Sie Tee **oder** Kaffee? *Would you like tea or coffee?*

Kommst du mit, **oder** bleibst du zu Hause? *Are you coming with us or staying at home?*

Mutti strickte, **und** Vati schlief. *Mummy was knitting, and Daddy was asleep.*

Er setzte sich hin **und** fing an zu lesen. *He sat down and began to read.*

Peter **und** Helga wohnen in Essen. *Peter and Helga live in Essen.*

Er ist nicht Deutscher **sondern** Schweizer.   *He is not German but Swiss.*

Er wartete nicht, **sondern** ging sofort aus dem Haus.   *He did not wait, but left the house immediately.*

Note that *sondern* must be used only when a preceding negative is categorically contradicted and replaced by its opposite: **nicht** *a* **sondern** *b* represents two mutually exclusive notions; *not old but quite young* calls for **sondern**, whereas *not old but quite experienced* calls for **aber**.

The other main class of conjunctions are called subordinating conjunctions because they introduce a subordinate clause, i.e. one which could not form a sentence on its own, but which depends upon the main clause. These conjunctions send the verb to the end of the clause. In other words the verb is always the last element of a subordinate clause. The chief subordinating conjunctions are **als** *when*, **bevor** *before*, **bis** *until*, **da** *as, since*, **damit** *in order that*, **daß** *that*, **indem** *while*, **nachdem** *after*, **ob** *whether*, **obgleich**, **obwohl** *although*, **seitdem** *since* (time, not cause), **während** *while*, **weil** *because*, **wenn** *if, whenever*, **wie** *how* and **wo** *where*. Examples:

Ich habe sie gesehen, **als** ich in Hamburg war.   *I saw her when I was in Hamburg.*

Ich habe ihn gesehen, **bevor** er nach Rom abreiste.   *I saw him before he left for Rome.*

Ich werde warten, **bis** er zurückkommt.   *I shall wait until he comes back.*

Da er es schon wußte, sagte er nichts.   *Since he knew that already, he said nothing.*

Er trat hervor, **damit** alle ihn sehen könnten.   *He stepped forward, so that they could all see him.*

Ich wußte, **daß** er nicht kommen wollte.   *I knew he didn't want to come.*

Indem ich dieses schreibe, spielt er mit dem Hund.   *As I write, he is playing with the dog.*

Er verabschiedete sich, **nachdem** er gegessen hatte.   *He took his leave after he had eaten.*

Ich weiß nicht, **ob** er kommt.   *I don't know whether he is coming.*

Obgleich es geregnet hatte, war es immer noch sehr warm.   *Although it had rained, it was still very hot.*

Seitdem er in Köln wohnt, sehe ich ihn nicht mehr.   *Since he's been living in Cologne, I don't see him any more.*

Ich höre gern Musik, **während** ich arbeite.   *I like listening to music while I work.*

Ich bin hier, **weil** man mich eingeladen hat. *I am here because I was invited.*

O gewiß, **wenn** ich darf. *Oh certainly, if I may.*

Er besucht uns immer, **wenn** er in London ist. *He always visits us when he's in London.*

Er ist schon weg, **wie** ich sehe. *He has already gone, as I see.*

Ich weiß, **wo** er wohnt. *I know where he lives.*

In addition to co-ordinating and subordinating conjunctions, there is a class of adverbial conjunctions, which are adverbs performing the function of connecting clauses together. When they introduce a clause, the order of subject and verb is inverted, for example:

Es ist zu spät; **außerdem** bin ich müde. *It's too late; besides, I'm tired.*

The commonest adverbial conjunctions are **also** *so, therefore*, **auch** *also, in addition*, **außerdem** *besides*, **daher**, **darum** *therefore*, **dann** *then*, **dennoch** *nevertheless, yet*, **deshalb**, **deswegen** *for that reason*, **inzwischen** *meanwhile*, **jedoch** *however*, **kaum** *scarcely*, **so** *so*, **sonst** *otherwise*, **trotzdem** *nevertheless*, **übrigens** *after all, by the way*. Examples:

Ich denke, **also** bin ich. *I think, therefore I am.*

Auch möchte ich darauf hinweisen, daß . . . *In addition I should like to draw attention to the fact that . . .*

Ich kann nicht kommen, **außerdem** habe ich kein Geld. *I can't come, anyhow I have no money.*

Es wiegt eine Tonne, **daher** brauchen wir einen Kran. *It weighs a ton, so we need a crane.*

Er wollte das Geld, **darum** hat er's gemacht. *He wanted the money, that's why he did it.*

Kauf diesen, **dann** wirst du zwei haben. *Buy this one, then you'll have two.*

Es ist unglaublich, **dennoch** ist es wahr. *It is incredible, nevertheless it is true.*

Das Leben ist teuer, **deshalb** müssen wir sparen. *Life is dear, so we must economise.*

Er ist erkältet, **deswegen** kommt er nicht. *He has a cold, that is why he hasn't come.*

Wir plauderten, **inzwischen** war die Sonne untergegangen. *We were chatting, meanwhile the sun had gone down.*

Er war ganz reich, **jedoch** war er nicht zufrieden. *He was quite rich, yet he wasn't content.*

Kaum war ich im Haus, als das Gewitter losbrach. *I was hardly in the house when the storm broke.*

Er sprach sehr leise, **so** konnte ich nichts verstehen. *He spoke very quietly, so I couldn't understand anything.*

Ich muß jetzt gehen, **sonst** komme ich zu spät. *I must go now, otherwise I'll be late.*

Ich hatte alles versucht, **trotzdem** ging es nicht. *I had tried everything, but it wouldn't work.*

Übrigens wäre ich froh, wenn sie es möglichst bald machen könnten. *Moreover I should be pleased if they could do it as soon as possible.*

Finally there is a class of correlative conjunctions, which go in pairs, like *neither . . . nor* in English. The commonest of these are **entweder . . . oder** *either . . . or*, **je . . . je/desto/um so** *the more . . . the more*, **nicht nur . . . sondern auch** *not only . . . but also*, **so . . . so** *as . . . as*, **weder . . . noch** *neither . . . nor* and **zwar . . . aber/doch** *indeed . . . but*:

Entweder du bleibst hier, **oder** du kommst mit. *Either you stay here or you come with us.*

Je mehr er hat, **je** mehr er will. *The more he has, the more he wants.*

Je länger ich bleibe, **desto** schwieriger wird es, aufzubrechen. *The longer I stay, the harder it becomes to leave.*

Nicht nur will sie es haben, **sondern** sie will mich **auch** zwingen, den Preis zu bezahlen. *Not only does she want it, she wants to force me to pay the price.*

So steinreich er ist, **so** geizig ist er auch. *He is as stingy as he is loaded.*

Weder wollte er länger bleiben, **noch** konnte er weggehen. *He neither wanted to stay any longer, nor was he able to get away.*

Zwar hat er nicht viel Geld, **aber** er ist immerhin großzügig. *It's true he hasn't a lot of money, but he's generous all the same.*

Zwar kam er, **doch** war es zu spät. *He did indeed come, but it was too late.*

Note that after **je** the second element may be **je, desto** or **um so**: they are more or less interchangeable; also that normal and inverted order of subject and verb are sometimes both found, the difference of meaning conveyed being one too subtle to bother with at this stage. The order given in the above examples is always safe.

In trying to decide which is the appropriate German equivalent for an English conjunction, problems most often occur with *as, that, then, therefore* and *when*:

as may be a conjunction of time (*As I was walking down the street*) = **als** or **während**, of manner (*As I see*) = **wie**, or of reason (*As he is the only one who knows*) = **da** or **weil**. It may also, of course, be an adverb (**so** or **ebenso**), and in comparisons of equality *as tall as I* is **so groß wie ich**. Note also *as a teacher, as an Englishman*: **als Lehrer, als Engländer**.

that as a conjunction may mean *in order that* = **damit**, or *with the result that* = **so daß**, otherwise it is **daß**, but it may also be an adjective = **dieser/jener**, or a pronoun = **das**.

then as a conjunction is **dann**, but it may also be an adjective (*the then prime minister* is **der damalige Ministerpräsident**) or an adverb (*I was then in London* is **Ich war damals in London**).

Of the various words for *therefore*, **daher** is the most objective, meaning *with the result that* and introducing a statement of the effect of the cause given in the preceding clause. **darum** is less objective but more emphatic, meaning *that is why*, and **deshalb** and **deswegen**, which are interchangeable, indicate only in a vague way that one thing is the result of another, meaning *that being so*, or *on that account*.

when as a conjunction is rendered by **wann** in indirect questions, e.g. **Ich weiß nicht, wann ich nach Hause komme**. *I don't know when I'm coming home*.; by **als** referring to a single event or state in the past, e.g. **Als ich ihn sah, war er sehr beschäftigt**. *When I saw him he was very busy*., **Als ich jung war, las ich viel**. *When I was young I read a lot*.; and by **wenn** referring to the present or future or to a repeated occurrence in the past, e.g. **Wenn mein Onkel uns besuchte, bekam ich immer schöne Geschenke**. *Whenever my uncle visited us I got lovely presents*. **Ich werde es ihm sagen, wenn er kommt**. *I'll tell him when he comes*.

This chapter has shown how conjunctions can affect word order; the next two will consider some principles governing word order in general.

23 Word Order – Position of Verb

The order in which words are placed within a sentence or clause is a topic of some complexity, which in German is best approached by first considering the position of the verb. Here there are three possibilities: the finite verb may be the second element in the sentence, as is most frequently the case, so that this is often called normal order; the verb may be the first element, as in many questions, for example; or it may be the last element, as in subordinate clauses.

The simplest case of normal word order is a sentence containing subject, verb and direct object, and nothing else, e.g. *I'll buy the car*. It is worth noting that German is more flexible than English here, and will equally accept **Ich kaufe das Auto** and **Das Auto kaufe ich**. The important point is that the verb must be the second element and cannot come in first or third position. Any other element may be stressed by being placed at the beginning, but the subject will jump to third position so that the verb remains second:

Heute **fährt** Peter in die Stadt. *Today Peter drives to town.*

Dort **kauft** er einige Bücher. *He buys a few books there.*

Dann **fährt** er nach Hause. *Then he drives home.*

This inversion of subject and verb is extremely common, occurring as it does in any main clause which does not begin with the subject; this includes any sentence which begins with a subordinate clause, which then counts as the first element:

Als ich ihn sah, **saß** er im Garten. *When I saw him he was sitting in the garden.*

Daß sie verheiratet war, **wußte** er nicht. *He did not know that she was married.*

There are, however, a number of parenthetical expressions which may be put at the beginning of a sentence without causing inversion. They are followed by a comma or exclamation mark, and are felt as standing outside the sentence. They include **Ja**, **Nein** and the name or other designation of the person addressed:

Ja, das stimmt. *Yes, that's right.*

Nein, er kann nicht. *No, he can't.*

Paul, wo ist dein Buch? *Paul, where's your book?*

Herr Lehrer, ich habe es vergessen. *I've forgotten it, teacher.*

The commonest of the other terms which qualify for this non-inversion treatment are (remember they are followed by a comma or exclamation mark): **also** *well now, well then,* **das heißt** *that is –* abbreviated in writing to **d.h.** = *i.e.*), **im Gegenteil** *on the contrary,* **mit anderen Worten** *in other words,* **nun** *well,* **na** *well,* **siehst du** *do you see,* **so** *well now, well then* and **unter uns** *between ourselves.*

The only circumstances where a subordinate clause may employ normal word order is in indirect speech and other noun clause objects when **daß** is not used. In other words *He thought that I was ill.* has subordinate clause word order in German: **Er glaubte, daß ich krank wäre.**, whereas *He thought I was ill.* will have normal word order: **Er glaubte, ich wäre krank**.

The verb occupies the first position in the sentence in most simple questions and commands, and in conditional clauses if **wenn** is omitted. Examples:

Kommst du mit in die Stadt? *Are you coming to town with me/us?*

Bleiben Sie hier oder gehen Sie mit den anderen? *Are you staying here or going with the others?*

Werden wir bald nach Hause gehen? *Are we going home soon?*

Bring' dein Heft hierher! *Bring your exercise book here!*

Gehen Sie zur Post und fragen Sie dort! *Go to the Post Office and ask there!*

Nehmen Sie bitte Platz! OR Bitte, nehmen Sie Platz! *Please take a seat!*

Hätte ich es nur gewußt! *If only I had known!*

Schreibst du ihr heute, dann bekommt sie den Brief morgen. *If you write to her today, she'll get the letter tomorrow.*

Before subordinate clause word order is dealt with, it should perhaps be pointed out that some grammars would differentiate the alternatives presented so far in a different way, dividing them according to whether the subject is the first element in the sentence ('normal order') or not ('inverted order'). I prefer to treat the position of the finite verb, whether as second element ('normal order') or as first element ('inverted order') as determinant, but must stress that a great variety of elements may bring about inversion of the 'first subject, then verb' order. The first element may, for example, be:

  (i) an infinitive:

    Zuhören mußt du, immer zuhören.   *You must listen, always listen.*

  (ii) an infinitive phrase:

    Um sie vom Bahnhof abzuholen, nahm ich den Wagen.   *I took the car to fetch her from the station.*

  (iii) an adverb of time, manner or place:

    Heute/Schnell/Dorthin muß er reiten.   *He must ride today/quickly/there.*

  (iv) an interrogative adverb:

    Warum sind die meisten Schauspieler arbeitslos?   *Why are most actors out of work?*

  (v) an adverbial clause:

    Wenn es ihm gelingt, kriegt er viel Geld.   *If he succeeds, he'll get a lot of money.*

  (vi) a prepositional phrase:

    Auf dem Lande haben wir ruhige Tage verbracht.   *We spent peaceful days in the country.*

  (vii) a past participle:

    Geschrieben ist es noch nicht.   *It's not written yet.*

  (viii) a complement:

    Ein treuer Freund bleibt er mir immer.   *He's still a faithful friend to me.*

  (ix) an adjectival phrase referring to the subject:

    Gehorsam wie ein Kind, ging er die Treppe hinauf.   *He went upstairs obedient as a child.*

  (x) a noun clause object:

    Daß er so faul war, hatte ich nicht erwartet.   *I hadn't expected him to be so lazy.*

In subordinate clause word order, the finite verb is the final item, coming after other items which are themselves normally the last element, such as dependent infinitives, past participles and separable prefixes. This is best demonstrated by showing the position of these last three elements in normal word order, and then transforming the examples into subordinate clauses:

Ich **muß** dieses Buch **lesen**.   *I must read this book.*

Mein Vater **hat** es **gesagt**.   *My father said so.*

Er **spricht** seine Meinung **aus**.   *He is expressing his opinion.*

Ich weiß, daß ich dieses Buch **lesen muß**.   *I know that I must read this book.*

Ich weiß, daß mein Vater es **gesagt hat**. *I know that my father said so.*

Ich weiß, daß er seine Meinung **ausspricht**. *I know that he is expressing his opinion.*

Although the above three are all noun clauses, the word order is, of course, the same in relative clauses:

Meine Mutter, die ganz ermüdet **war**, ging früh zu Bett. *My mother, who was quite tired out, went to bed early.*

and adverbial clauses:

Er konnte nicht bezahlen, weil er kein Geld **hatte**. *He could not pay, because he had no money.*

Two cases have been noted where the verb does not go to the end in a subordinate clause: the first is in indirect statements without **daß**, and the second is in *even if* or *as if* conditional clauses with **wenn** omitted. The third and only other exception may be irreverently termed the Great German Subordinate Clause Pile-Up, and refers to occasions which produce verbal log-jams such as:

Ihr Chef tadelte sie, weil sie mir einen Brief hätte schicken lassen sollen. *Her boss told her off, because she ought to have had a letter sent to me.*

These multiple verb groups in subordinate clauses always involve modal auxiliaries which, as will be recalled from Chapter 16, use their infinitive form with past participle function in compound tenses – that is why there appear to be three consecutive infinitives in the above admittedly exceptional example. The version with three verbs, the finite one coming first, is less uncommon:

Du kannst ihn daran erinnern, daß er mir einen Brief wird schreiben müssen. *You can remind him that he will have to write me a letter.*

The rule is that if a subordinate clause contains an infinitive and a modal past participle (which is, of course, infinitive in form), the auxiliary does not come last but precedes these two, i.e. the modal verb comes last, the infinitive before that, and the auxiliary verb (whether **haben** or **werden**) comes first in the multiple verb group. A few more examples may help to drive the pattern home:

Wenn ich hätte kommen wollen, wäre ich auch gekommen. *If I had wanted to come, I should have done so.*

Ich muß Ihnen leider mitteilen, daß das Endspiel hat verschoben werden müssen. *Unfortunately I must inform you that the final has had to be postponed.*

Es war klar, daß er nicht würde weitergehen können. *It was clear that he would not be able to go any further.*

The position within a sentence of non-finite parts of the verb has in part already been touched upon in noting that infinitives, infinitive phrases and past participles may be the first element in a sentence; they may implicitly be anywhere after the verb in normal order. Participial phrases, i.e. groups of words formed around a present or past participle, are extremely common and function as parentheses, having no effect upon the word order. The following are some of the commonest, though it should be noted that in general participles are much less used in German than in English:

genau genommen   *strictly speaking*
ehrlich gesagt   *honestly speaking*
im Grunde genommen   *basically*
wie erwartet   *as expected*
rein praktisch gesehen   *from a purely practical point of view*

The present participle is much rarer, being often rendered in German by a clause, thus *She sat in her room ceaselessly knitting.* is **Sie saß in ihrem Zimmer und strickte unaufhörlich**, not **unaufhörlich strickend**.

While dependent infinitives and past participles normally come last, as in

Ich werde es morgen noch einmal versuchen.   *I shall try again tomorrow.*
Ich habe es ihm versprochen.   *I've promised it to him.*

When a sentence ends with both an infinitive and a past participle, the one on which the other depends comes last – this applies to all the sentences with modal verbs as well:

Er hat mich schwimmen gelehrt.   *He has taught me to swim.*
Er hat nicht kommen können.   *He has been unable to come.*

Having examined at some length the position of the verb within the sentence, since it may fairly be considered the keystone or linch-pin of the sentence, we may turn our attention in the next chapter to the position of other elements such as objects, adverbial elements and pronouns.

24 Word Order – Other Elements

Within the framework imposed by the fixed position of the verb, short words and small items tend to come early in the sentence, while long words and lengthier groups tend to come towards the end. A good example of this is the little word **sich**, the position of which is often puzzling to the English student.

In a main clause without inversion the reflexive pronoun usually follows immediately after the verb:

Man kann sich nichts Schöneres vorstellen. *One can imagine nothing more beautiful.*

In a main clause with inversion it precedes a noun subject but follows a pronoun subject:

Jetzt freuen sich die Kinder auf Weihnachten. *Now the children are looking forward to Christmas.*

Jetzt freuen sie sich auf Weihnachten. *Now they are looking forward to Christmas.*

In a subordinate clause the reflexive pronoun comes as soon as possible after the conjunction or relative pronoun, yielding pride of place only to a pronoun subject:

Es ist kaum zu erwarten, daß sich die Lage verbessern wird. *It is hardly to be expected that the situation will improve.*

Es ist kaum zu erwarten, daß sie sich verbessern wird. *It is hardly to be expected that it will improve.*

In an infinitive phrase the reflexive pronoun comes first:

Sie bat ihn, sich auf die Bank hinzusetzen. *She asked him to sit down on the bench.*

Ich befahl ihm, sich in den nächsten Tagen gründlich über die technischen Voraussetzungen des neuen Verfahrens zu informieren. *I instructed him to familiarise himself thoroughly in the next few days with the technical requirements of the new process.*

Pronoun objects, whether direct or indirect, normally precede all adverbial expressions:

Wir haben ihn heute morgen in der Stadt gesehen. *We saw him in town this morning.*

Es war ihm längst von seinem Vater versprochen worden. *It had been promised to him by his father a long time ago.*

They also precede noun objects or even noun subjects:

Ich habe es meiner Schwester gezeigt. *I showed it to my sister.*

Heute hat ihn mein Vater gesehen. *My father saw him today.*

As noted in Chapter 8, when there are two objects, if both are nouns, the indirect precedes the direct; if both are pronouns, the direct precedes the indirect; and if one is a noun and the other a pronoun, the pronoun always comes first:

Er zeigte seinem Lehrer das Buch. *He showed the book to his teacher.*

Er zeigte ihm das Buch. *He showed him the book.*

Er zeigte es seinem Lehrer. *He showed it to his teacher.*

Er zeigte es ihm. *He showed it to him.*

Note, however, that either the direct or indirect object may be placed in initial position if it is desired to stress it:

Meinem Vater schenkte er die kostbarsten Schätze. *It was to my father that he presented the greatest treasures.*

Mich kann niemand anklagen. *Nobody can accuse **me**.*

A complement, as distinct from an object proper, tends to occupy a later position:

Sein Freund wurde zehn Jahre später in Wien Generaldirektor. *His friend became managing director in Vienna ten years later.*

Where a sentence contains several adverbial elements, the order: time – reason – manner – place applies in general:

Wir sind gestern wegen des Regens schnell nach Hause zurückgekommen. *We came back home quickly yesterday because of the rain.*

The following points should be noted concerning the position of an adverbial element with respect to other parts of the sentence:

In a sentence with two noun objects an adverbial element will stand between them:

Wir haben unseren Freunden schnell Auf Wiedersehen gesagt. *We quickly said goodbye to our friends.*

An adverbial element precedes a noun object or a pronoun object after a preposition:

> Ich spiele oft mit meinen Freunden im Park Fußball. *I often play football in the park with my friends.*
>
> Er hat noch nie mit mir gesprochen. *He has never yet spoken to me.*

unless the adverbial element is really a complement to the verb:

> Er hat die Maschine in Gang gebracht. *He got the machine going.*
>
> Er hat viele Gedichte auswendig gelernt. *He learned many poems off by heart.*

These adverbs are felt as part of the verb, almost like a separable prefix; cf. **Deutsch sprechen** *to speak German*, **die Macht ergreifen** *to seize power*.

An adverbial element precedes a predicative adjective, contrary to English usage.

> Mein alter Onkel ist seit Weihnachten krank. *My old uncle has been ill since Christmas.*
>
> Du siehst mit dieser neuen Brille komisch aus. *You look funny in those new spectacles.*

The above remarks indicate the normal position of adverbial elements, but where it is desired to emphasise a particular adverbial element, this is achieved by placing it anywhere other than in its normal position:

> Nächste Woche werde ich vielleicht Zeit haben, jetzt aber nicht. *I may perhaps have time next week, but not at the moment.*
>
> Die Mannschaft hat gut in Hamburg gespielt, aber nicht in Mailand. *The team played well in Hamburg, but not in Milan.*

Those adjectives which govern the dative case normally follow the dative noun or pronoun dependent on them. The commonest of these are: **bekannt** *acquainted*, **dankbar** *grateful*, **fremd** *unknown*, **gleich** *similar*, **nah(e)** *near*, **schuldig** *guilty, owing*, **treu** *faithful*, **willkommen** *welcome*, **verbunden** *obliged* – likewise **unbekannt, undankbar, untreu**, etc.

> Diese Ausgabe ist mir unbekannt. *I don't know this edition.*
>
> Ich bin Ihnen dafür sehr verbunden. *I'm much obliged to you for that.*
>
> Er war ihr sehr dankbar. *He was very grateful to her.*
>
> Sie war dem Weinen nahe. *She was near to tears.*

nicht is placed immediately before the expression which it negates:
> Er wußte nicht, was er tun sollte.   *He didn't know what to do.*
> Es war nicht schlecht, nachts zu arbeiten.   *It wasn't bad working at night.*

Where **nicht** applies to the statement as a whole it comes last, except for an infinitive, a past participle, a predicative noun or adjective or a separable prefix:
> Das ist nicht richtig – es ist nicht dein Haus, siehst du das nicht?   *That's not right – it's not your house, can't you see that?*

nicht may also be placed before an adverb of manner or place:
> Er hat nicht fleißig gearbeitet und ist heute nicht in der Schule.   *He hasn't been working hard and isn't at school today.*

Note that *not a* is frequently **kein** and not **nicht ein**:
> Du bist doch kein Kind mehr.   *You're not a child any more.* BUT
> Könnte ich nicht ein Zimmer für mich haben?   *Couldn't I have a room to myself.*

Although an adverbial element cannot normally come between subject and verb, words for *however* (**aber**, **jedoch**, **dagegen**, **indessen**) constitute an exception to this rule:
> Die Eltern aber blieben zu Hause.   *The parents, however, stayed at home.*
> Ich dagegen setzte meine Hoffnung auf Herrn X.   *I, however, put my hope in Mr. X.*

A noun subject is often postponed to the end of the clause; this gives it added emphasis, though with verbs of happening it has almost become the norm:
> Gestern ereignete sich um 4 Uhr in der Königsallee ein Verkehrsunfall.   *There was a traffic accident in the Königsallee yesterday at four o'clock.*
> Letzte Woche hat mich leider niemand besucht.   *Unfortunately nobody at all visited me last week.*
> Ich glaube, daß morgen in der Schule eine kleine Feier stattfinden soll.   *I believe there is to be a little celebration at school tomorrow.*

It is worth making the point that these various points concerning word order are not purely arbitrary, but reflect the relative importance of the respective elements; thus the most unemphatic and least obtrusive position in a sentence is immediately after the finite verb in normal word order, and this is occupied by pronouns, since they refer to persons or things already named, and needing no emphasis may precede adverbial and noun elements – if for any reason a pronoun does need emphasising, it is moved to a more prominent position in the sentence. Similarly the reason a complement comes last in a simple sentence is because it is important:

> Ich war nach dem Militärdienst sieben Jahre in Bonn Studienrat. *After military service I was a secondary school teacher in Bonn for seven years.*

Finally it should be observed that considerations of euphony may be allowed to alter word order on occasion, and many of the rules are breached in colloquial German – there is no need to be afraid of them!

The concluding chapter of this book will be devoted to highlighting those points from the preceding chapters which are most frequently the occasion for mistakes on the part of English learners.

25 Key Points Recapitulated

This final chapter sets out to mention once more not the pivotal and most important features of German grammar (such as declensions or strong verbs), but simply those points where English learners most commonly trip up.

Among the differences between English and German in the use of articles, the one which English students seem to find most forgettable is the German omission of an indefinite article when indicating occupation or nationality, so that one does not say in German *I am a teacher*, *He is an American*, but **Ich bin Lehrer**, **Er ist Amerikaner**.

For any noun there are four things one must know: its gender, whether it is weak, like **der Junge** *the boy*, **der Mensch** *the human being*, whether it is an adjective masquerading as a noun, like **der Beamte** *the civil servant*, **der Deutsche** *the German*, and what is its plural ending.

Among pronouns it is relatives which cause the greatest difficulties; they agree with the noun they stand for in gender and number, but not in case: this is determined by the function (e.g. as subject or object) of the relative pronoun within its clause. Thus **Ich habe einen Freund, der Polizist ist**. *I have a friend who is a policeman.*, **Mein Freund, den wir heute treffen, hat ein neues Auto**. *My friend, whom we are meeting today, has a new car.* Don't forget that relative pronouns can never be left out in German as they so often are in English: **Eine Frau, die ich kenne, hat es selbst gesehen**. *A woman I know saw it herself.* Remember also that the comma, which in English basically indicates a pause and is often discretionary, is strictly a grammatical marker in German and cannot be omitted between clauses except between co-ordinate clauses joined by *und* and having the same subject:

Er verabschiedete sich und ging sofort nach Hause. *He took his leave and went home immediately.*

Der Freund, der es mir gab, sagte, daß es zehn Mark kostete. *The friend who gave it to me said it cost ten marks.*

The use of personal pronouns also includes some pitfalls; there is no easy way of knowing when a reflexive pronoun, for example, is accusative or dative. In general it is either a direct object and therefore accusative, as in **Ich wasche mich** *I wash myself* or a dative of possession, as in **Ich wasche mir die Hände** *I wash my hands*, but the dative reflexive occurs idiomatically, as in **Ich will mir das Haus ansehen** *I'm going to have a look at the house* and **Er hat es sich notiert** *He's made a note of it* – one can only await the growth of one's own **Sprachgefühl** and be thankful that this particular point is not a crucial one. More important is the constant concentration the foreigner must apply whenever the words **sie** (*she, it, they*) **Sie** (*you*) and their other cases occur, since real confusion can arise from misunderstanding, even more in speech than in writing, where the capital letters on the 'you' forms are helpful.

The handling of numbers in German is associated with two types of mistake which are common. The first is easy to avoid: it concerns only the spelling and pronunciation of a very small number of numerals which do not conform exactly to the general pattern. These are the ones incorporating any of the following: **dreißig** *thirty*, **sechzehn** *sixteen*, **sechzig** *sixty*, **siebzehn** *seventeen* and **siebzig** *seventy*. The second concerns the order in which the components of a complex number are presented. Here German is the odd man out among the major languages: the number *thirty-two*, for example, is *trente-deux* in French, *trentadue* in Italian, *treinta y dos* in Spanish, *tridtsat' dva* in Russian, but in German it is **zweiunddreißig**, i.e. all one word and the wrong way round to boot. This causes one of the most frequently occurring mistakes which English learners make, when they both say and understand fifty-seven when in fact seventy-five is meant – if the English learner remembers 'four and twenty blackbirds baked in a pie' as the German pattern, this can help.

English words ending in *-ing* mislead students of German more often than any other verbal form; whereas the present participle or gerund in *-ing* serves a great variety of purposes in English, the German equivalent will be a present participle in **-end** only when it is used adjectivally or adverbially, e.g. **ein lachendes Kind** *a laughing child*, **ein schneidend kalter Wind** *a cuttingly cold wind*. In other words, for an English word in *-ing* another construction is usually needed in German. This may be any of the following:

(i) an infinitive with **zu**, particularly after the prepositions **anstatt** and **ohne**:

Anstatt ins Kino zu gehen, fuhr er nach Hause.   *Instead of going to the cinema he drove home.*

Er ging weiter, ohne mich zu sehen. *He walked on without seeing me.*

Es hat aufgehört zu schneien. *It has stopped snowing.*

(ii)   an infinitive without **zu** after **bleiben, finden, hören, lehren, lernen, sehen:**

Er blieb stehen. *He remained standing.*

Er fand die Hefte auf dem Tisch liegen. *He found the exercise books lying on the table.*

Ich höre ihn kommen. *I hear him coming.*

Er lehrte mich schwimmen. *He taught me swimming.*

Jetzt lernt sie singen. *Now she's learning singing.*

Wir sahen ihn kommen. *We saw him coming.*

(iii)   a subordinate clause introduced by a conjunction:

Bevor er zu Bett ging, machte er das Licht aus. *Before going to bed he switched the light off.*

Nachdem wir geschwommen waren, waren wir alle sehr müde. *After swimming we were all very tired.*

(iv)   **und** + verb:

Sie stand da und lachte. *She stood there laughing.*

(v)   a relative clause:

Der Mann, der da liegt, ist verletzt. *The man lying there is wounded.*

(vi)   **bei** + infinitive as a noun:

Vorsicht beim Einsteigen! *Take care getting in!*

Sie ist beim Ankleiden. *She's getting dressed.*

Sprich nicht beim Essen! *Don't talk when you're eating!*

Expressions of time include one or two stumbling-blocks. Whereas in English we refer to a year by saying, for example, *In nineteen eighty-six*, in German one must not say **In neunzehnhundertsechsundachtzig** but either **Im Jahre neunzehnhundertsechsundachtzig** or simply **neunzehnhundertsechsundachtzig**. In print, of course, such a date more often appears in figures:

Beethoven wurde 1770 geboren. *Beethoven was born in 1770.*

Im Jahre 1939 brach der zweite Weltkrieg aus. *The Second World War broke out in 1939.*

When nouns like morning, evening, Sunday are used adverbially they no longer have a capital letter: **heute morgen** *this morning*, **gestern abend** *last night*, **sonntags** *on Sundays*. And remember that **halb drei** is *half past two*, not *half past three*!

Many English verbs have more than one meaning, and the student needs to be aware of this in order to select the appropriate German verb; only the very commonest can be mentioned here: thus *to ask for something* is **bitten um**; *to ask whether, what, etc.* is **fragen**:

Er bat mich um etwas Schreibpapier.   *He asked me for some writing paper.*

Er fragte mich, was das bedeute.   *He asked me what that might mean.*

gehen is normally *to go on foot, to walk*; **fahren** is *to go by vehicle. To meet* is usually **treffen**; **begegnen** stresses that it is a chance encounter, and **abholen** is used for meeting someone off a train or plane, or collecting someone from home, theatre etc.

to put: **legen** is *to lay*; **stellen** is *to stand*; **stecken** is *to insert*:

Er legte das Buch auf den Tisch.   *He put the book on the table.*

Er stellte die Flasche auf den Tisch.   *He put the bottle on the table.*

Er steckte die Hand in die Tasche.   *He put his hand in his pocket.*

Watch out for verbs which are reflexive in German but not in English, such as:

sich anziehen *to dress*   sich erkälten *to catch cold*
sich fühlen *to feel – intrans.* sich rasieren *to shave*
sich setzen *to sit down*   sich treffen *to meet*
sich waschen *to wash – intrans.*

The most important rule of word order is that the main verb stands as the second idea in the sentence:

Ich kaufe heute etwas für dich in der Stadt.   *I'll buy you something in town today.*

Heute kaufe ich etwas für dich in der Stadt.

In der Stadt kaufe ich etwas für dich heute.

Etwas für dich kaufe ich heute in der Stadt.

Wenn ich in der Stadt bin, kaufe ich etwas für dich.

In the last example the whole subordinate clause counts as the first idea.

The conjunctions **aber, denn, oder, sondern** and **und** do not affect the word order; all other conjunctions send the verb to the end.

Pay particular attention to the position of separable prefixes:

Ich gehe früh aus.   *I go out early.*

Ich ging früh aus.   *I went out early.*

but in a subordinate clause:

Wenn ich früh ausgehe . . .   *If I go out early . . .*

Als ich früh ausging.   *When I went out early.*

perfect tense; infinitive with **zu**:

Ich bin früh ausgegangen.   *I went out early.*

Ich brauche, früh auszugehen.   *I need to go out early.*

Remember that in a subordinate clause introduced by **daß**, the **daß** may be omitted, in which case the subordinate clause will revert to main clause word order:

> Er glaubte, daß die Deutschen immer pünktlich seien./Er glaubte, die Deutschen seien immer pünktlich. *He believed (that) the Germans were always punctual.*

These are the chief problem areas which most frequently cause difficulties, but of course they yield in importance to the need to know one's adjective endings and verb conjugations. Learning those is the real slog of mastering German grammar, but the thing to bear constantly in mind is that in every moment's encounter with the language something rubs off, provided you have the motivation to learn. You will learn correct German by seizing every chance to use it, every moment on the bus or elsewhere to peruse a page of this book, every occasion you have to listen either to German language programmes on the BBC or to German radio itself, every opportunity which arises to see a German film, to meet a German, and of course every possibility of visiting West or East Germany, Austria or Switzerland. Every public library has elementary German readers as well as masterpieces of German literature – many a learner has begun his acquaintance with the latter through a story by Theodor Storm called *Immensee*, which has the incomparable virtue of being short! Remember, a little more is absorbed on every encounter with the language, and little and often is a good motto.

Appendix I   The Sounds of German

Although German uses the same alphabet as English, very few of the letters always represent exactly the same sound in both German and English. It may fairly be said, however, that the sounds represented by the letters *f*, *k*, *m*, *n*, *p*, *t* and *x* are to all intents and purposes the same in both languages, though a trained phonetician might perhaps notice a slight difference in some cases. It is worth familiarising oneself with the symbols used to represent the sounds in the International Phonetic Alphabet, since most dictionaries indicate the pronunciation by means of these symbols, which are usually identified by being printed between square brackets thus [   ]. The phonetic symbols corresponding to the sounds which occur in German are as follows:

Vowels

All vowels may be long or short; in phonetic transcription a colon after the symbol indicates that the vowel is long. As a rule of thumb one may say that vowels in unstressed syllables are short, as are vowels followed by two or more consonants, although a silent *h* after a vowel makes it long. All other vowels are long, as are all diphthongs – but this is only a rough rule, and one should always be on the look out for exceptions. The sentences given below for practice purposes have been devised artificially and should not be taken as evidence that the German language is absurd – the medium is the message!

[a]   short, light, forward *a* in **Mann** (*man*), **kalt** (*cold*).
[a:]   long *a* in **Tat** (*deed*), **Abend** (*evening*).
Practise: Der Mann tanzt im Walde.   *The man is dancing in the forest.*
          Ja, sagt der Vater.   *Yes, says the father.*
[ɛ]   short, open *e* or *ä* in **Bett** (*bed*), **Hände** (*hands*).

[ɛ:]   long ditto in **ähnlich** (*similar*).

[ə]   short open mid-vowel in **genau** (*exactly*), **alle** (*all*) – always unstressed.

[e]   long, tight *e* in **Tee** (*tea*), **fehlt** (*is missing*).

Practise: Ich nehme den Weg zum See.   *I take the path to the lake.*
Städte wie Essen haben schlechtes Wetter.   *Towns like Essen have bad weather.*
Alle Straßen haben einen kleinen Laden.   *All streets have a small shop.*

[i]   long *ee* in **mir** (*me*), **Liter** (*litre*), also spelt *ie* in **nie** (*never*), **hier** (*here*).

[ɪ]   short, open *i* in **mit** (*with*), **ist** (*is*).

Practise: Wir spielen ihm die Lieder.   *We play him the songs.*
Im Winter sitze ich hinter dem Tisch.   *In winter I sit behind the table.*

[o:]   long, closed *o* in **Oper** (*opera*), **ohne** (*without*).

[ɔ]   short, open *o* in **oft** (*often*), **offen** (*open*).

Practise: Zu Ostern wohnt die Oma einen Monat im Hotel.   *Grandma lives in the hotel for a month at Easter.*
Im Sommer kommt Onkel Wolfgang vom Osten.   *In summer Uncle Wolfgang comes over from the east.*

[ø:]   long, closed *ö* in **hören** (*to hear*), **böse** (*angry*).

[œ]   short, open *ö* in **können** (*can*), **öffnen** (*to open*).

Practise: Wir hören die Söhne stöhnen.   *We hear the sons groaning.*
Plötzlich nicken die Köpfe der Töchter aus Köln.   *Suddenly the heads of the daughters from Cologne nod.*

[y:]   long, closed *ü* in **über** (*over*), **süß** (*sweet*).

[ʏ]   short, open *ü* in **Glück** (*luck*), **müssen** (*must*).

Practise: Die Brüder der Schüler fühlen sich müde.   *The schoolboys' brothers feel tired.*
Frau Müller läßt ein Fünfmarkstück im Münster.   *Frau Müller leaves a five mark piece in the Minster.*

[u:]   long, closed *oo* in **tun** (*to do*), **Juni** (*June*).

[ʊ]   short, open *u* in **und** (*and*), **hundert** (*hundred*).

Practise: "Du ruderst gut" ruft Rudi.   *"You row well" cries Rudy.*
Der Hund hat Hunger und ißt ein Pfund Wurst.   *The dog is hungry and eats a pound of sausage.*

Semi-vowels and diphthongs

[j]   This symbol is used to represent the normal pronunciation of the German letter *j*, which sounds like the English *y* in *yes*, and is termed a semi-vowel because, although it does not function like

a vowel in a syllable, it is formed like a vowel with no interruption of the free passage of air from the vocal chords, e.g. **jung** (*young*).

[ai] This symbol represents the diphthong in the English word *kite*, and has four spellings in German, *ai, ay, ei, ey*: **Mai** (*May*), **Bayern** (*Bavaria*), **mein** (*my*), **Meyer** (*Meyer*, a common proper name).

[au] This symbol represents the diphthong in **Haus** (*house*). It is slightly different from that in English *house*, in that its first element is *a* as in *father* and not *a* as in *back*: **Maus** (*mouse*), **Sau** (*sow*).

[ɔi] This symbol represents the diphthong in the English word *boil*, and has two spellings in German, *äu* and *eu*: **äußerst** (*extremely*), **neu** (*new*).

Practise: Ein Teil meines Kleids ist leider schmutzig. *One part of my dress is unfortunately dirty.*

Sie laufen aus dem Haus zum Auto hinaus. *They run out of the house to the car.*

Heute läuft der Verkäufer aus dem neuen Gebäude. *Today the salesman runs out of the new building.*

Consonants

[b] (i) voiced, as in English *babble*, when it is the first letter of a word or syllable, or when it is doubled: **bin** (*am*) [bIn], **Blick** (*glance*) [blɪk], **aber** (*but*) [aːbər], **Ebbe** (*ebb*) [ɛbə].

(ii) when *b* is the last letter of a word or syllable, or when it is, other than as an initial consonant, as in **bleiben** (*to stay*) [blaibn] or **bringen** (*to bring*) [brɪŋən], followed by another consonant, it becomes voiceless and is pronounced as *p*: **ob** (*whether*) [ɔp], **liebte** (*loved*) [liːptə], **Abfahrt** (*departure*) [apfaːrt].

[d] (i) voiced, as in English *do*, when it is the first letter of a word or syllable: **dann** (*then*) [dan], **oder** (*or*) [oːdər], **werde** (*become*) [vɛrdə].

(ii) When *d* is the last letter of a word or syllable, or when it is, other than as an initial consonant as in **drei** (*three*) [drai] or **draußen** (*outside*) [drausn], followed by another consonant, it becomes voiceless and is pronounced as *t*: **Hand** (*hand*) [hant], **endlich** (*finally*) [ɛntlɪç], **Tod** (*death*) [toːt].

[g] (i) voiced, as in English *gag*, when it is the first letter of a word or syllable: **Gast** (*guest*) [gast], **Auge** (*eye*) [augə], **groß** (*big*) [groːs].

(ii)   When *g* is the last letter of a word or syllable, except in the combinations **ng** and *ig*, it becomes voiceless and is pronounced as *k*: **Tag** (*day*) [taːk], **sorgfältig** (*carefully*) [zɔrkfɛltɪç], **wegnehmen** (*to take away*) [vɛkneːmən].

(iii) The combination *ng* is pronounced as in English *singer*, not as in English *finger*, and is represented by the phonetic symbol [ŋ]: **Angst** (*fear*) [aŋst], **Ding** (*thing*) [dɪŋ], **anfangen** (*to begin*) [anfaŋən].

(iv)   The suffix *ig* is pronounced as if it were *ich* and is represented by [ɪç] in phonetic script: **dreißig** (*thirty*) [draisɪç], **Schwierigkeit** (*difficulty*) [ʃviːrɪçkait], **fertig** (*ready*) [fɛrtɪç]. The pronunciation of this sound will be dealt with in more detail below.

Note: *b, d, g* are the only consonants which in final position change from voiced to voiceless.

[h]   at the beginning of a word or syllable is pronounced as in English *hit*: **haben** (*to have*) [haːbən], **gehoben** (*raised*) [gəhoːbən], **Gehalt** (*salary*) [gəhalt]. Elsewhere it serves to make the preceding vowel long and is not pronounced itself: **gehen** (*to go*) [geːn], **Ehe** (*marriage*) [eːə], **Fahrt** (*journey*) [faːrt], **sah** (*saw*) [zaː]. For its pronunciation in the combinations *ch*, *th*, and *sch* see below.

[l]   in German *l* is a much more forward sound than in English, with the tip of the tongue touching the front of the palate or even the upper teeth: **lieb** (*dear*) [liːp], **voll** (*full*) [fɔl].

[r]   This symbol represents an *r* trilled on the tongue, i.e. with the tip of the tongue vibrating against the centre of the palate, similar to the *r* in Italian, Spanish or Russian. Although it is quite acceptable in German, the commoner pronunciation is the *r* in the back of the throat, represented by the phonetic symbol [R]. Very often this sound is attenuated to a simple partial closure of the throat with no actual vibration. This sound is represented by the phonetic symbol [ʁ]. As all three sounds are acceptable, we shall for simplicity use only the first, i.e. [r], in this outline.

[s]   When *s* is the last letter of a word or syllable, or when it occurs before consonants, except initially before *p* or *t*, it is pronounced like the English *s* in *soap*. This sound is also represented by the symbol *ß* (see page 3): **als** (*when*) [als], **besser** (*better*) [bɛsər], **beste** (*best*) [bɛstə], **deshalb** (*therefore*) [dɛshalp], **groß** (*big*) [groːs].

[z]   When *s* is the first letter of a word or syllable and is followed by a vowel it is pronounced like the English *z* in *zoo*: **See** (*lake* or *sea*) [zeː], **so** (*so*) [zoː], **lesen** (*to read*) [leːzn], **Insel** (*island*) [ɪnzl], **diese** (*this*) [diːzə].

[ʃ] When *s* is the first letter of a word or syllable and is followed by *p* or *t* it is pronounced like the English *sh* in *sheep*: **Spiel** (*game*) [ʃpi:l], **Spaß** (*fun*) [ʃpa:s], **Stück** (*piece*) [ʃtʏk], **bestimmt** (*definitely*) [bəʃtɪmt], **Gespräch** (*conversation*) [gəʃprε:ç]. This sound is also represented by the combination *sch*: **schön** (*beautiful*) [ʃøn], **schnell** (*quick*) [ʃnεl], **Tisch** (*table*) [tɪʃ], **Geschichte** (*story*) [gəʃɪçtə].

[v] *w* is pronounced like the English *v* in *vat*: **wo** (*where*) [vo:], **gewesen** (*been*) [gəve:zn], **Entwicklung** (*development*) [εntvɪklʊŋ]. Note that the letter *v*, though pronounced as *v* in some words of foreign origin: **Vase** (*vase*) [va:zə], **Revolution** (*revolution*) [rεvɔlutsio:n], is normally pronounced as *f* in German: **von** (*from*) [fɔn], **viel** (*much*) [fi:l]

Complex consonants

q As in English, *q* occurs only when followed by *u*. *qu* is pronounced *kv*: **Quadrat** (*square*) [kvadra:t], **Qualität** (*quality*) [kvalɪte:t].

z The letter *z* is pronounced *ts*: **Zahl** (*number*) [tsa:l], **Zug** (*train*) [tsu:k], **inzwischen** (*meanwhile*) [ɪntsvɪʃn]. *tz* is also pronounced *ts*: **Satz** (*sentence*) [zats].

th *th* is pronounced as a simple *t*: **Theater** (*theatre*) [tea:tər], **Thema** (*theme*) [te:ma].

c The letter *c* on its own is found only in foreign words – if these are thoroughly assimilated into German it is replaced by either *z* or *k*: **Zigarette** (*cigarette*) [tsɪgarεtə], **Kaffee** (*coffee*) [Kafe:]. If it occurs before *e* or *i* it is pronounced *ts*, as in **circa** (*approximately*) [tsɪrka], **Cis** (*C sharp* in music) [tsɪs]. Otherwise it is pronounced *k*, as in **Café** (*café*) [kafe:], **Camping** (*camping*) [kεmpɪŋ].
   ck is also pronounced *k*: **dick** (*fat*) [dɪK], **schmeckt** (*tastes*) [ʃmεkt].

ph is pronounced *f*: **Physik** (*physics*) [fyzi:k], **Phantasie** (*fantasy*) [fantazi:].

ch after *a*, *o* or *u*, *ch* is pronounced as in the Scottish word *loch*, a guttural sound. This sound is represented by the phonetic symbol [x]: **acht** (*eight*) [axt], **Loch** (*hole*) [lɔx], **Buch** (*book*) [bu:x], **auch** (*also*) [aux], after *e*, *i* or a consonant it is pronounced rather like the English *h* in *hew*, *huge*. This sound is represented by the phonetic symbol [ç]: **Licht** (*light*) [lɪçt], **recht** (*right*) [rεçt], **weich** (*soft*) [vaiç], **welche** (*which*) [vεlçə], **Furcht** (*fear*) [fʊrçt], **bißchen** (*bit*) [bɪsçən], **Brötchen** (*bread roll*) [brøtçən]. This pronunciation is also used after modified vowels *ä, ö* and *ü* and the diphthongs *eu, äu*: **Gedächtnis** (*memory*) [ɡədɛçtnɪs], **Löcher** (*holes*) [lœçər], **flüchten** (*flee*) [flʏçtən], **leuchten** (*to shine*) [lɔiçtən].

ch is pronounced *k* in certain loan words and in stem syllables where it is followed by *s*: **Charakter** (*character*) [karaktər], **Chlor** (*chlorine*) [kloːr], **Christ** (*Christian*) [krɪst], **Fuchs** (*fox*) [fʊks], **wachsen** (*to grow*) [vaksən].

ch is pronounced as *sch*, i.e. like English *sh*, in some foreign words: **Chance** (*opportunity*) [ʃãsə], **Chef** (boss) [ʃɛf].

x   Although *x* was included in the initial list of consonants identical with English, all the others of which have phonetic symbols corresponding to their normal form (*f, k, m, n, p, t*), it should be pointed out that *x* is a complex consonant and is in fact pronounced *ks*: in phonetic transcription it is therefore represented by [ks].

[ʒ]   This symbol represents the *s* in English *pleasure*. It is not strictly speaking a German sound, but is given here because it occurs in a number of words of foreign (usually French) origin as a pronunciation of either *g* or *j*: **Etage** (*storey*) [etaːʒə], **Garage** (*garage*) [garaːʒə], **Ingenieur** (*engineer*) [inʒeniøːr], **Jalousie** (*Venetian blind*) [ʒaluziː], **Journal** (*magazine*) [ʒʊrnaːl].

It is not to be expected that the reader will absorb this large and rather indigestible catalogue of pronunciation rules at one sitting: brief but frequent reference back to it is the recommended procedure. At this point it is worth reflecting that not all the instances which differ from English can really be termed difficult. For instance, it may seem rather eccentric of the Germans to pronounce *b* as *p* at the end of a word, just as it may appear odd that whereas they quite sensibly pronounce a short *i* as in *blip*, they pronounce a long one as in *bleep* and not as in *like*. Such differences, however, can hardly be regarded as presenting insuperable obstacles, but will undoubtedly be mastered with a little practice. It is advisable to give extra attention to those sounds which, because they simply do not occur in English, can be said to present real difficulties. Foremost among these are the *ch* and *r* sounds, together with the long *ü* and some other vowels.

Most people when gargling use their vocal chords, producing sounds of varying acceptability. One may, however, without impropriety, practise gargling without using the vocal chords. The result will infallibly be the German hard *ch* (generally called the **ach** sound). If one then precedes it with an *ah*, we need never again hear the Englishman saying 'Ack! Ack!' instead of **Ach! Ach!**

If one resumes the gargling practice, this time using the vocal chords, the result is in fact the guttural *r* sound [R]. In other words [R] might be described as a voiced [x]. Perhaps this is the sound represented by strip-cartoonists as "Aaargh!" Conversely the **ach** sound [x] could be described as a breathed or voiceless [R].

The soft *ch* sound (generally known as the **ich** sound) was described as resembling the English *h* in *huge*. The key to getting it right is to have the sides of the rear of the tongue *between* the back teeth, i.e. lightly gripped by them. This differentiates it completely from [ʃ], in which the back teeth come together, and from the h in *Hugh*, in which the rear edges of the tongue do not spread so far as to be *between* the back teeth.

Even when these difficult *ch* and *r* consonant sounds have been mastered, the tell-tale English *l* may stick out like a sore thumb. It is normally pronounced with the tongue much farther back than in the German *l*, which is sometimes said to resemble the English *l* in *leek*, that word having an *l* as far forward as an English *l* ever gets, but the German *l* has the tongue even farther forward. It is advisable to exaggerate it and put the tip of the tongue right against the upper teeth. The difference may be practised with English *Billy* and German **billig**.

The long *ü* vowel [y:] is produced by tightly rounding the lips and pushing them out, meanwhile trying to say *ee* [i:]. Thus English *green* if said with protruding rounded lips (as for whistling) will give its German equivalent **grün**.

In general it must be emphasised that German vowels are pure, i.e. they could theoretically be prolonged indefinitely with no change of sound from start to finish, unlike English vowels, many of which are diphthongs, e.g. *cake* is [keik], *kite* is [kait], *most* is [moust]. The long *e* [e:] is sometimes said to resemble a long *a* in northern English; it is, to be more precise – for the difference is an important one – much more like the sound in the Tyneside pronunciation of *Blaydon Races* (a sound which will be familiar to most readers, if only from numerous popular television series) than the sound in the Yorkshire or Lancashire pronunciation of *a rainy day today*, which inclines more to [ε]. If [e:] is pronounced with rounded lips the result is [ø:]. These are the sounds which give the English student the most trouble, and it is well worth giving them extra practice.

The point made earlier that vowels in unstressed syllables are short is not helpful unless one is able to identify which syllables are stressed and which unstressed. There is an erroneous idea around that stress in English and German falls on the initial syllable, but belief in this misconception will induce the unwary beginner to commit untold varieties of mistakes. Consider the preceding observation attentively.

In fact the stress tends in most cases to fall on the root or stem syllable, and never on, for example, an inseparable prefix. In the following examples, syllables to be stressed are marked in bold.

Words which exemplify this basic rule include **Al**ter *age*, **än**dern *to alter*, Be**fehl** *command*, ver**lor**en *lost*, Ge**dan**ke *thought*.

In compounds the stress is on the component which is most important for the meaning: Auf**merk**samkeit *attention*, **Geg**enteil *contrary*.

Many foreign words, particularly French ones, are stressed as in their original language: Ak**zent** *accent*, Bü**ro** *office*, Ca**fé** *café*, Kon**zert** *concert*.

The suffixes **-anz, -at, -ei, -ieren, -ik, -ist, -tät, -tion** and **-ur** are nearly always stressed: Ele**ganz** *elegance*, Tole**ranz** *tolerance*, Sa**lat** *salad*, Zi**tat** *quotation*, Arz**nei** *medicament*, Poli**zei** *police*, pro**bier**en *to sample*, interes**sier**en *to interest*, Kri**tik** *criticism*, Repu**blik** *republic*, Kompo**nist** *composer*, Poli**zist** *policeman*, Elektrizi**tät** *electricity*, Quali**tät** *quality*, Infek**tion** *infection*, Na**tion** *nation*, Fi**gur** *figure*, Tempera**tur** *temperature*.

Although it is usual to speak of stress as falling on one syllable or another, it is of course the vowel in that syllable which bears the stress, and one does not speak of stressed or unstressed consonants, so that from that point of view it does not much matter where one syllable ends and another begins. Where this does matter, however, is when occasion arises to split a word, for example in typewriting. If in a two-syllable word there is only one consonant between the vowels, it will go with the second syllable on the second line, e.g. **ge-ben, Va-ter, Bru-der**; if a number of consonants represent in fact a single sound, they are not divided, e.g. **la-chen, wa-schen**, but *ck* is printed as *k-k*: **Dek-kel, guk-ken**. If the first syllable consists of a vowel on its own, the word is never divided: **aber, eher**. Compound words are divided into their component parts: **Donners-tag, Markt-platz**.

This does not claim to be an exhaustive treatment of syllabification, as the subject is not one about which detailed knowledge is necessary to competent performance in German except for typesetters and some linguist typists. Like stress, it is an appendage, though a less important one, to the detailed outline of pronunciation rules which, of course, is of paramount importance.

Appendix II   The Structure of the German Vocabulary

This appendix will begin by considering some regular correspondences between certain consonants in German words and certain other consonants in their English equivalents. It will show how German words are built up from smaller component parts, thus going from the building-bricks which together constitute each syllable (i.e. letters of the alphabet) to the building-bricks which together form whole words (i.e. roots, prefixes and suffixes). The purpose of this is to put you in a position to make a more informed guess at the meaning of a German word you are meeting for the first time.

No English speaker learning German can fail to notice that English words beginning with *th* tend to begin in German with *d* – **drei** *three*, **der** *the*, **du** *thou* and so on. This is an example of a phenomenon known to linguists as the Second Sound Shift (**zweite Lautverschiebung**), which occurred only in German (more strictly termed High German) and distinguishes it from all the other languages in the Germanic family (which could collectively be referred to as Low German languages – the sub-group to which English belongs). It took place during the dark ages, for reasons not fully understood and which are the subject of controversy. It affected most of the sounds in the language, but only a handful of examples will be mentioned here, as being particularly useful in deducing meaning from form.

Primitive Germanic initial *t* became High German *z*: **zu** *too*, **zehn** *ten*, **Zoll** *toll*. Sometimes it is not quite so obvious as in these examples, when other sounds in the word have markedly changed, or there has been a change of meaning: **ziehen** *to tug*, **zahm** *tame*, **zählen** *to count*, but originally *to tell*, cf. tellers in Scottish banks or House of Commons votes. Two common German nouns we have not used in this book are **die Zunge** and **der Zweig**. Can you guess their meanings? You can check them in the vocabulary.

Initial *d* became *t*: **tun** *to do*, **Tochter** *daughter*, **trinken** *to drink*. Less obvious examples include **Tag** *day*, **teuer** *dear*, **träumen** *to dream*. We have not yet met the verb **tanzen** or the noun **der Tropfen**. Can you work out their meaning?

Initial *th* became *d*: **Dank** *thanks*, **dein** *thine*, **Ding** *thing*. Less obvious examples include **Dach** *roof* = *thatch*, **daß** *that*, **denken** *to think*, **durch** *through*. Can you work out the meaning of **der Durst** and the adjective **dünn**?

Initial *p* became *pf*: **Pfennig** *penny*, **Pfeife** *pipe*, **Pfund** *pound*. Less obvious examples include **Pfad** *path*, **Pfahl** *pole*, **Pfanne** *pan*. Can you work out the meanings of the verbs **pflanzen** and **pflücken**?

These correspondences do not apply to every word beginning with the initial consonant in question, for many such words have entered the language since the Second Sound Shift took place, but they are sufficiently reliable to be worth bearing in mind with most new words. You will find they sometimes apply even when the consonants concerned are not initial ones, e.g. **Herz** *heart*, **unter** *under*, **Bruder** *brother*, **Kupfer** *copper*, a fact which is worth remembering – did you get **Tropfen** and **pflanzen** right? Three sound changes which apply to consonants in medial or final position in the word now follow.

p became *f*: **offen** *open*, **helfen** *to help*, **scharf** *sharp*. Less obvious examples include **auf** *up*, **hoffen** *to hope*, **Schlaf** *sleep*, **Waffen** *weapon*. Can you work out the meanings of **der Affe** and **der Pfeffer**?

t became *s* (*ß, ss*): **besser** *better*, **beißen**, *to bite*, **aus** *out*. Less obvious examples include **essen** *to eat*, **groß** *great*, **Straße** *street*, **vergessen** *to forget*. Can you work out the meaning of **hassen** and **das Wasser**?

k became *ch*: **Buch** *book*, **machen** *to make*, **rechnen** *to reckon*. Less obvious examples include **brechen** *to break*, **sprechen** *to speak*, **suchen** *to seek*, **Woche** *week*. Can you work out the meaning of **der Becher** and **kochen**?

These changes in medial and final consonants do not apply in every case – *ch* in German often corresponds to a silent *gh* in English, for example (**Licht, Nacht, durch, dachte** and so on), but they are frequent enough to be useful. Any history of the German language will tell you more about the Second Sound Shift, if this section has whetted your appetite; it has been kept very brief in case it has turned your stomach.

Turning now to the formation of nouns, it is obvious that some monosyllables are pure roots themselves, e.g. **Hand** *hand*, **gut** *good*, but that the number of these is necessarily limited. Most German nouns are formed from simple roots either by compounding them or by means of prefixes and/or suffixes.

Compound nouns join two or more words, of which the last must be a noun. The most obvious type is when two nouns are simply stuck together: **der Fuß + der Ball = der Fußball** (as in English); **der Markt + der Platz = der Marktplatz** – the meaning is crystal clear. Where the two nouns joined are different in gender, the compound noun always has the gender of the final component: **der Mittag + das Essen = das Mittagessen** *lunch, midday meal*, **das Obst + die Torte = die Obsttorte** *fruit flan*. This process can produce some exceedingly long compound nouns; we have met **die Geschwindigkeit** *speed* and **beschränken** *to limit*, and so **die Geschwindigkeitsbeschränkung** *speed limit* should not be difficult to work out: the trick is to examine the separate components and work out that, for example **das Flughafengebäude** must mean *the airport terminal building*.

Compared with English, German has a much higher proportion of compound nouns formed from Germanic components, and correspondingly fewer formed from Greek and Latin elements; this has the effect of making the German words' meaning more obvious: in linguistic terminology they are 'transparent', where the Greek and Latin derivatives are 'opaque'. Thus in German, *equilibrium* is **das Gleichgewicht** ('equal weight'), *compassion* is **das Mitleid** ('with-suffering'), *suicide* is **der Selbstmord** ('self-murder'), *circumstance* is **der Umstand** ('the around-standing'), and *duel* is **der Zweikampf** ('two-struggle'). This transparency in German extends beyond our Greek and Latin derivatives: what could **der Fingerhut** ('finger hat') be but a *thimble*, or **der Handschuh** ('hand-shoe') but a *glove*?

When nouns are compounded, a linking letter *s* or *(e)n* is often inserted: **die Lebensversicherung** *life assurance*, **die Straßenecke** *street corner*. Note particularly that, although feminine nouns never inflect in the singular, an *s* is nevertheless regularly added in compounds to feminine nouns ending in -**heit**, -**keit**, -**schaft**, -**ung**, -**ion** and -**tät**: **der Freiheitskrieg** *war of independence*, **das Minderwertigkeitsgefühl** *inferiority complex* – 'lesser worthiness feeling', **die Gesellschaftslehre** *sociology*, **die Meinungsumfrage** *opinion poll* – 'opinion asking-around', **die Religionsgeschichte** *history of religion*, **die Qualitätskontrolle** *quality control*.

As mentioned above, although the final component of a compound noun must itself be a noun, the earlier components may be other parts of speech: **die Abreise** *departure* – 'off journey', **das Unterseeboot** (abbr. **U-Boot**) *submarine*, **der Edelwein** *wine of superior quality*, **die Untertasse** *saucer* – 'under cup'. Nevertheless the majority of compound nouns are indeed formed solely from nouns. There are also compound adjectives – **scheinheilig** *sanctimonious*, **naßkalt** *cold and wet* – but they are a much smaller and less important category.

There are between thirty and forty common suffixes which, when added to a root, turn it into a particular part of speech, usually, in fact, changing one part of speech into another. Thus the suffix **-bar** forms adjectives: **Dank** is *thanks* and so **dankbar** is *thankful* or *grateful*; **essen** is *to eat* and **eßbar** is *edible*. Suffixes which form adjectives in this way include **-bar**, **-(e)n**, **-ern**, **-haft**, **-ig**, **-isch**, **-lich**, **-los**, **-mäßig**, **-reich**, **-sam** and **-voll** – a round dozen in all.

-bar often corresponds to English *-able* or *-ible* when added to verb stems and to English *-ful* when added to nouns: **erreichbar** *attainable* = *reachable*, **erkennbar** *recognisable*, **furchtbar** *frightful*, **wunderbar** *wonderful*.

-(e)n and **-ern** denote the substance something is made of: **golden** *gold*, **eisern** *iron*, **gläsern** *glass*, **silbern** *silver*.

-haft may be added to nouns, verbs or other adjectives: **heldenhaft** *heroic*, **sagenhaft** *legendary*, **krankhaft** *morbid*.

-ig means 'having the nature or characteristics of', and often corresponds to an English adjective ending in *-y*: **blutig** *bloody*, **durstig** *thirsty*, **saftig** *juicy*.

-isch sometimes corresponds to English *-ish*, is used for adjectives of nationality, and is the commonest suffix for adjectives based on foreign words: **kindisch** *childish*, **englisch** *English*, **österreichisch** *Austrian*, **französisch** *French*, **akademisch** *academic*, **historisch** *historic*, **musikalisch** *musical*.

-lich (English *-like*, *-ly*) may be added to nouns, adjectives or verbs: **freundlich** *friendly*, **kindlich** *child-like*, **herbstlich** *autumnal*, **kleinlich** *petty*, **rötlich** *reddish*, **begreiflich** *comprehensible*, **sterblich** *mortal*, **tödlich** *deadly*.

-los corresponds to English *-less*: **arbeitslos** *unemployed*, **haarlos** *hairless*, **geruchlos** *odourless*, **hoffnungslos** *hopeless*.

-mäßig means *in accordance with*: **planmäßig** *according to plan*, **gewohnheitsmäßig** *habitual*, **vorschriftsmäßig** *correct, as prescribed*.

-reich means *rich in*: **glorreich** *glorious*, **kinderreich** *with many children*, **einflußreich** *influential*, **hilfreich** *helpful*.

-**sam** (English -*some*): **einsam** *lonely, lonesome,* **langsam** *slow,* **ratsam** *advisable,* **gemeinsam** *joint, common,* **schweigsam** *taciturn.*

-**voll** (English -*ful*): **gedankenvoll** *thoughtful,* **geheimnisvoll** *mysterious,* **hoffnungsvoll** *hopeful,* **wertvoll** *valuable.*

Other suffixes form adverbs; among the commonest of these are -**s**, -**weise**, -**halb**, -**wärts**, -**e** – it should be borne in mind, of course, that virtually all adjectives may be used as adverbs too.

-**s** may be added to adjectives or nouns to form an adverb, e.g. **anders** *otherwise,* **besonders** *especially,* **links** *on the left,* **rechts** *on the right,* **anfangs** *in the beginning,* **abends** *in the evening,* **morgens** *in the morning,* **nachmittags** *in the afternoon,* **nachts** *at night.*

-**weise** may be added to adjectives or nouns to form an adverb: **teilweise** *partly,* **glücklicherweise** *fortunately,* **komischerweise** *funnily enough,* **normalerweise** *in the normal course of events,* **beispielsweise** *by way of example,* **ausnahmsweise** *by way of exception,* **schrittweise** *step by step*; note that **er** is inserted when adding -**weise** to an adjective, but **s** only sometimes when adding it to a noun: **kreuzweise** *crosswise, crossways* but **versuchsweise** *tentatively, by way of experiment.*

-**halb** forms such adverbs as **außerhalb** *outside,* **innerhalb** *inside, within,* **oberhalb** *above,* **unterhalb** *below.*

-**wärts** (English *ward(s)*) in **abwärts** *downward(s),* **auswärts** *outward(s),* **seitwärts** *sideway(s),* **rückwärts** *backward(s),* **vorwärts** *forward(s).*

-**e** is an archaic adverbial suffix which survives in just a few very common words such as **gerne** *gladly,* **nahe** *nearby,* **lange** *long,* which are preferred to the more modern forms **gern**, **lang** and **nah** more often than not.

The following suffixes serve to form nouns: -**e**, -**ei**, -**el**, -**er**, -**heit**, -**keit**, -**ling**, -**nis**, -**schaft**, -**sel**, -**tum**, -**ung** – once again a round dozen:

-**e** added to adjective stems denotes the quality itself. It may also be added to verb stems – **die Breite** *width,* **die Ferne** *distance,* **die Höhe** *height,* **die Kälte** *cold,* **die Bitte** *request,* **das Ende** *end,* **die Lage** *situation.*

-**ei**: **die Arznei** *medicament,* **die Druckerei** *printing works,* **die Partei** *political party,* **die Polizei** *police.*

-el: **der Deckel** *lid*, **das Drittel** *third*, **der Engel** *angel*, **der Löffel** *spoon*, **der Nebel** *mist*, **der Vogel** *bird*.

-er usually indicates the occupation or function of the person designated, but may also simply indicate origin from a particular place: **der Anhänger** *supporter*, **der Ausländer** *foreigner*, **der Bäcker** *baker*, **der Fahrer** *driver*, **der Leiter** *leader*, **der Maler** *painter*, **der Berliner** *Berliner*.

-heit forms feminine abstract nouns from adjectives: **die Einzelheit** *detail*, **die Freiheit** *freedom*, **die Gelegenheit** *opportunity*, **die Gesundheit** *health*, **die Gewohnheit** *habit*, **die Wahrheit** *truth*.

-keit is used instead of -heit with adjectives ending in -bar, -ig, -lich or -sam: **die Dankbarkeit** *gratitude*, **die Schwierigkeit** *difficulty*, **die Freundlichkeit** *kindness, friendliness*, **die Aufmerksamkeit** *attention*.

-ling: **der Flüchtling** *refugee*, **der Frühling** *spring*, **der Lehrling** *apprentice*, **der Zwilling** *twin* – this suffix has something of the diminutive, pitying associations of English 'princeling', 'foundling', 'duckling'.

-nis is added to verbal stems: **die Erlaubnis** *permission*, **das Hindernis** *hindrance*, **die Kenntnis** *knowledge*, **das Verhältnis** *relationship*, **das Zeugnis** *evidence*.

-schaft (English -ship) denotes collectives or states: **die Gemeinschaft** *community*, **die Gesellschaft** *society*, **die Mannschaft** *team*, **die Freundschaft** *friendship*, **die Bereitschaft** *readiness*.

-sel: **das Rätsel** *puzzle*, **der Schlüssel** *key*, **die Schüssel** *dish*, **das Überbleibsel** *remnant*.

-tum: **das Christentum** *Christianity*, **das Eigentum** *property*, **der Irrtum** *error*, **der Reichtum** *riches*.

-ung is very common indeed, forming feminine abstract nouns from verb stems: **die Forschung** *research*, **die Hoffnung** *hope*, **die Lösung** *solution*, **die Meinung** *opinion*, **die Ordnung** *order*, **die Sammlung** *collection*, **die Wohnung** *apartment* – many other examples have occurred in this book.

In terms of the sheer number of words they engender, prefixes are even more productive than suffixes, largely because of the huge number of verbs which are formed by adding a separable or inseparable prefix; these, however, were specifically dealt with in Chapter 15, and will not further be touched upon here.

Apart from the immensely fruitful rôle of prefixes in forming verbs, their chief function is in the formation of nouns. The commonest noun prefixes are **Ge-, Miß-, Mit-, Rück-, Un-, Ur-** and **Wohl-**. To these seven should be added three prefixes which are themselves nouns: **Grund-** (*basic*), **Haupt-** (*head, chief, main*) and **Spitzen-** (*peak*).

Ge-: this very productive prefix forms three types of nouns in about equal numbers; collective nouns (which have umlaut where possible): **das Gepäck** *luggage*, **das Geräusch** *sound*, **das Geschirr** *crockery*, **das Geschrei** *shouting*; nouns formed from verbal stems and signifying the product of the verb, as it were: **der Gedanke** *thought*, **der Gehalt** *content, capacity*, **der Geruch** *smell*, **der Gesang** *song*, **der Geschmack** *taste*; and nouns falling into neither of these categories: **die Geburt** *birth*, **die Geschichte** *story, history*, **das Gesetz** *law*, **das Gesicht** *face*. See Vocabulary for a further score of examples.

Miß- indicates the opposite of the word it is prefixed to: **der Mißbrauch** *misuse*, **der Mißerfolg** *failure*, **die Mißhandlung** *ill-treatment*, **das Mißverständnis** *misunderstanding*.

Mit- usually signifies being together: **der Mitarbeiter** *colleague, workmate*, **das Mitglied** *member*, **das Mitleid** *sympathy*, **der Mitreisende** *fellow traveller*.

Rück- has the basic meaning of *back*: **der Rückblick** *retrospect, glance back*, **die Rückfahrt** *return journey*, **die Rückkehr** *return*, **der Rücksitz** *back seat*.

Un- is prefixed to nouns to signify the opposite: **die Unabhängigkeit** *independence*, **das Unglück** *misfortune*, **die Unordnung** *disorder*, **die Unruhe** *unrest*.

Ur- signifies origin and beginnings: **die Uraufführung** *first performance*, **die Urkunde** *title deed, document*, **die Ursache** *cause*, **der Ursprung** *source, origin*, **die Urgroßmutter** *great-grandmother*.

Wohl- denotes the good or agreeable: **die Wohlfahrt** *welfare*, **das Wohlsein** *well-being*, **der Wohlstand** *prosperity*, **das Wohlwollen** *goodwill*.

Grund- used as a prefix adds the sense of *basic*: **die Grundlage** *basis*, **der Grundsatz** *principle*, **die Grundschule** *elementary school*, **die Grundzahl** *cardinal number*.

Haupt- adds the sense of *head, chief, main*: **der Hauptbahnhof** *main station*, **der Hauptmann** *Captain*, **die Hauptsache** *main thing*, **die Hauptstadt** *capital city*.

Spitzen- adds the sense of *peak* or *maximum*: **die Spitzengeschwin-digkeit** *maximum speed*, **die Spitzenleistung** *peak output*, *best perform-ance*, **das Spitzenwert** *peak value*, **die Spitzenzeiten** (pl.) *peak period, rush hours*.

It is hoped that these observations on how German words are formed and how they relate to English parallels will alert the learner to the possibilities of building one's vocabulary without total dependence on a dictionary.

Appendix III   List of strong verbs

The following list is not complete, but includes the commonest strong and irregular verbs. The two vowels at the head of each group indicate the stem vowels of the simple past tense and past participle respectively of the verbs in that group.

Group I – a, e

Infinitive	3rd Sing. Present	3rd. Sing. Simple Past	3rd Sing. Perfect	
bitten	bittet	bat	hat gebeten	*to ask*
essen	ißt	aß	hat gegessen	*to eat*
fressen	frißt	fraß	hat gefressen	*to eat* (of animals)
geben	gibt	gab	hat gegeben	*to give*
geschehen	geschieht	geschah	ist geschehen	*to happen*
lesen	liest	las	hat gelesen	*to read*
liegen	liegt	lag	hat gelegen	*to lie*
messen	mißt	maß	hat gemessen	*to measure*
sehen	sieht	sah	hat gesehen	*to see*
sitzen	sitzt	saß	hat gesessen	*to be sitting*
treten	tritt	trat	ist getreten	*to step*
vergessen	vergißt	vergaß	hat vergessen	*to forget*

Group II – a, o

befehlen	befiehlt	befahl	hat befohlen	*to order*
beginnen	beginnt	begann	hat begonnen	*to begin*
brechen	bricht	brach	hat/ist gebrochen	*to break*
empfehlen	empfiehlt	empfahl	hat empfohlen	*to recommend*
erschrecken	erschrickt	erschrak	ist erschrocken	*to be frightened*
gelten	gilt	galt	hat gegolten	*to be valid, worth*
gewinnen	gewinnt	gewann	hat gewonnen	*to win*
helfen	hilft	half	hat geholfen	*to help*
nehmen	nimmt	nahm	hat genommen	*to take*
schwimmen	schwimmt	schwamm	ist geschwommen	*to swim*
sprechen	spricht	sprach	hat gesprochen	*to speak*

Infinitive	3rd Sing. *Present*	3rd. Sing. *Simple Past*	3rd Sing. *Perfect*	
stechen	sticht	stach	hat gestochen	*to sting*
stehlen	stiehlt	stahl	hat gestohlen	*to steal*
sterben	stirbt	starb	ist gestorben	*to die*
treffen	trifft	traf	hat getroffen	*to meet*
verderben	verdirbt	verdarb	hat verdorben	*to spoil*
werfen	wirft	warf	hat geworfen	*to throw*

Group III – a, u

binden	bindet	band	hat gebunden	*to tie*
finden	findet	fand	hat gefunden	*to find*
gelingen	gelingt	gelang	ist gelungen	*to succeed*
klingen	klingt	klang	hat geklungen	*to sound*
singen	singt	sang	hat gesungen	*to sing*
sinken	sinkt	sank	ist gesunken	*to sink*
springen	springt	sprang	ist gesprungen	*to jump*
trinken	trinkt	trank	hat getrunken	*to drink*
verschwinden	verschwindet	verschwand	ist verschwun- den	*to disappear*
zwingen	zwingt	zwang	hat gezwungen	*to force*

Group IV – i, i

beißen	beißt	biß	hat gebissen	*to bite*
gleiten	gleitet	glitt	ist geglitten	*to slide*
greifen	greift	griff	hat gegriffen	*to seize*
leiden	leidet	litt	hat gelitten	*to suffer*
pfeifen	pfeift	pfiff	hat gepfiffen	*to whistle*
reißen	reißt	riß	hat gerissen	*to tear*
reiten	reitet	ritt	ist/hat geritten	*to ride*
schneiden	schneidet	schnitt	hat geschnitten	*to cut*
schreiten	schreitet	schritt	ist geschritten	*to stride*
streiten	streitet	stritt	hat gestritten	*to argue*

Group V – ie, ie

bleiben	bleibt	blieb	ist geblieben	*to stay*
leihen	leiht	lieh	hat geliehen	*to lend*
reiben	reibt	rieb	hat gerieben	*to rub*
scheinen	scheint	schien	hat geschienen	*to shine, seem*
schreiben	schreibt	schrieb	hat geschrieben	*to write*
schreien	schreit	schrie	hat geschrieen	*to shout*
schweigen	schweigt	schwieg	hat geschwiegen	*to be silent*
steigen	steigt	stieg	ist gestiegen	*to climb*
treiben	treibt	trieb	hat getrieben	*to drive*
vermeiden	vermeidet	vermied	hat vermieden	*to avoid*

Infinitive	*3rd Sing.* *Present*	*3rd. Sing.* *Simple Past*	*3rd Sing.* *Perfect*	
verzeihen	verzeiht	verzieh	hat verziehen	*to pardon*
weisen	weist	wies	hat gewiesen	*to show*

Group VI – ie, a

blasen	bläst	blies	hat geblasen	*to blow*
braten	brät	briet	hat gebraten	*to roast*
fallen	fällt	fiel	ist gefallen	*to fall*
fangen	fängt	fing	hat gefangen	*to catch*
halten	hält	hielt	hat gehalten	*to hold, to stop*
hängen	hängt	hing	hat gehangen	*to hang*
lassen	läßt	ließ	hat gelassen	*to leave*
raten	rät	riet	hat geraten	*to advise*
schlafen	schläft	schlief	hat geschlafen	*to sleep*

Group VII – o, o

biegen	biegt	bog	hat gebogen	*to bend, turn*
bieten	bietet	bot	hat geboten	*to offer*
fliegen	fliegt	flog	ist geflogen	*to fly*
fliehen	flieht	floh	ist geflohen	*to flee*
fließen	fließt	floß	ist geflossen	*to flow*
frieren	friert	fror	hat gefroren	*to freeze*
genießen	genießt	genoß	hat genossen	*to enjoy*
gießen	gießt	goß	hat gegossen	*to pour*
heben	hebt	hob	hat gehoben	*to raise*
kriechen	kriecht	kroch	ist gekrochen	*to creep*
lügen	lügt	log	hat gelogen	*to tell lies*
riechen	riecht	roch	hat gerochen	*to smell*
schieben	schiebt	schob	hat geschoben	*to push*
schießen	schießt	schoß	hat geschossen	*to shoot*
schließen	schließt	schloß	hat geschlossen	*to shut*
schmelzen	schmilzt	schmolz	hat/ist geschmolzen	*to melt*
schwören	schwört	schwor	hat geschwören	*to swear*
verlieren	verliert	verlor	hat verloren	*to lose*
wiegen	wiegt	wog	hat gewogen	*to weigh*
ziehen	zieht	zog	hat gezogen	*to pull*

Group VIII – u, a

fahren	fährt	fuhr	ist gefahren	*to travel*
graben	gräbt	grub	hat gegraben	*to dig*
laden	lädt	lud	hat geladen	*to load*
schaffen	schafft	schuf	hat geschaffen	*to create*
schlagen	schlägt	schlug	hat geschlagen	*to hit*
tragen	trägt	trug	hat getragen	*to carry, to wear*

Infinitive	3rd Sing. Present	3rd. Sing. Simple Past	3rd Sing. Perfect	
wachsen	wächst	wuchs	ist gewachsen	*to grow*
waschen	wäscht	wusch	hat gewaschen	*to wash*

Group IX – a, a

brennen	brennt	brannte	hat gebrannt	*to burn*
bringen	bringt	brachte	hat gebracht	*to bring*
denken	denkt	dachte	hat gedacht	*to think*
kennen	kennt	kannte	hat gekannt	*to know*
nennen	nennt	nannte	hat genannt	*to name*
rennen	rennt	rannte	hat gerannt	*to run*
senden	sendet	sandte	hat gesandt	*to send*
		sendete	hat gesendet	
wenden	wendet	wandte	hat gewandt	*to turn*
		wendete	hat gewendet	

Group X – miscellaneous

gehen	geht	ging	ist gegangen	*to go*
haben	hat	hatte	hat gehabt	*to have*
heißen	heißt	hieß	hat geheißen	*to be called*
kommen	kommt	kam	ist gekommen	*to come*
laufen	läuft	lief	ist gelaufen	*to run*
rufen	ruft	rief	hat gerufen	*to call*
sein	ist	war	ist gewesen	*to be*
stehen	steht	stand	hat gestanden	*to stand*
stoßen	stößt	stieß	hat gestossen	*to knock*
tun	tut	tat	hat getan	*to do*
werden	wird	wurde	ist geworden	*to become*
wissen	weiß	wußte	hat gewußt	*to know*

All compounds of verbs in this list will conjugate according to the above pattern; thus **abnehmen** *to lose weight*, **sich benehmen** *to behave*, **entnehmen** *to take from* and **mitnehmen** *to take with one* will all conjugate like **nehmen**. Where a perfect tense is given with both auxiliaries, e.g. **hat/ist gebrochen**, **haben** is used when the verb is transitive and **sein** when it is intransitive.

Vocabulary

You have now met some 1500 of the commonest words in modern German – indeed 85 % of them can be found in Kosaras' *Grundwortschatz* which was mentioned in the Introduction, the remainder being words whose inclusion can be justified on various grounds – they illustrate an important point, are useful compounds of other words already mentioned, are of particular use to the English learner, and above all are very commonly used, even if not quite qualifying for membership of the magic 3,000 club. Here is a check list to assist your vocabulary acquisition. With strong verbs the vowel of the third person singular present tense is omitted where it does not differ from the infinitive.

ab *off, down, (away) from*
der **Abend** *evening*
abends *in the evening*
aber *but, however,*
abfahren (ä, u, ist abgefahren) *to depart, drive away*
die **Abfahrt** *departure*
abhängen (i, hat abgehangen) *to depend*
abholen *to fetch, collect*
abnehmen (i, a, hat abgenommen) *to take off, lose weight*
abonnieren *to subscribe (to)*
die **Abreise** *departure*
die **Absicht** *intention, purpose*
die **Abstammung** *descent*
abwärts *downwards*
die **Adresse** *address*
der **Affe** *ape*
ähnlich *similar*
der **Akzent** *accent*
das **Album** *album*
der **Alkohol** *alcohol*
all *all*
allerdings *indeed, of course*
allgemein *general*

als *than, as, when*
also *thus, so, consequently*
alt *old*
das **Alter** *age*
an *at, on, to*
anbieten (o, hat angeboten) *to offer*
andere *other*
ändern *to alter, change*
anders *otherwise, differently*
anerkennen (a, hat anerkannt) *to recognise, acknowledge*
anfangen (ä, i, hat angefangen) *to begin*
anfangs *at first, initially*
angenehm *pleasant, agreeable*
die **Angst** *fear, anxiety*
der **Anhänger** *supporter*
ankommen (a, ist angekommen) *to arrive*
die **Ankunft** *arrival*
der **Anruf** *telephone call*
anrufen (ie, hat angerufen) *to telephone, ring up*
der **Anschein** *appearance*
ansehen (ie, a, hat angesehen) *to look at, consider*

anstecken *to light (e.g. a cigarette)*
anvertrauen *to entrust*
(sich) anziehen (o, hat angezogen) *to dress, put on, pull*
der **Apfel** *apple*
die **Apfelsine** *orange*
der **April** *April*
die **Arbeit** *work*
arbeiten *to work*
arbeitslos *out of work, unemployed*
(sich) ärgern *to annoy (be annoyed)*
arm *poor*
der **Arm** *arm*
die **Arznei** *medicament, medicine*
der **Arzt** *male doctor*
die **Ärztin** *woman doctor*
atmen *to breathe*
auch *also, too, even*
auf *on, to*
aufbrechen (i, a, hat/ist aufgebrochen) *to break up*
die **Aufmerksamkeit** *attention*
(sich) aufregen *to excite (get excited)*
die **Aufregung** *excitement*
das **Auge** *eye*
der **Augenblick** *moment*
aus *out of, from*
der **Ausdruck** *expression*
die **Ausgabe** *edition*
ausgehen (i, ist ausgegangen) *to go out*
der **Ausländer** *foreigner*
ausmachen *to matter, settle, switch off*
die **Ausnahme** *exception*
ausnahmsweise *exceptionally*
außen *outside*
außer *with the exception of, outside*
äußer *outer, exterior*
außerdem *besides*
außerhalb *outside*
äußerst *extreme(ly)*
aussprechen (i, a, hat ausgesprochen) *to express, pronounce*
ausverkaufen *to sell out*
der **Ausweg** *way out*

auswendig *by heart*
(sich) ausziehen (o, hat ausgezogen) *to undress, take off*
das **Auto** *the motor car*

das **Baby** *baby*
der **Bäcker** *baker*
das **Bad** *bath*
der **Bahnhof** *railway station*
bald *soon*
der **Band** *book, volume*
das **Band** *ribbon, bond*
die **Bank** *bench, Bank*
bauen *to build*
die **Baumwolle** *cotton*
der **Bayer** *Bavarian*
Bayern (n.) *Bavaria*
beabsichtigen *to intend*
der **Beamte** *civil servant*
beantworten *to answer*
beaufsichtigen *to supervise*
der **Becher** *beaker*
die **Bedingung** *condition, precondition*
sich beeilen *to hurry*
der **Befehl** *order, command*
befehlen (ie, a, hat befohlen) *to order, command*
begegnen *to meet*
begierig *eager*
beginnen (a, hat begonnen) *to begin*
begreifen *to understand, grasp*
behaupten *to assert*
die **Behörde** *authority*
bei *near, with, at*
beide *both*
das **Bein** *leg*
das **Beispiel** *example*
beispielsweise *by way of example*
beißen (i, hat gebissen) *to bite*
bekannt *known, acquainted*
der/die **Bekannte** *acquaintance*
bekanntlich *as is well known*
bekommen (a, hat bekommen) *to get, receive, obtain*
beleuchten *to illuminate*
die **Beleidigung** *insult*

sich **benehmen** *to behave*
die **Bereitschaft** *readiness*
der **Berg** *hill, mountain*
der **Bericht** *report*
berühmt *famous, renowned*
beschäftigen *to occupy, employ*
beschließen (o, hat beschlossen) *to resolve*
(sich) **beschränken** *to limit, restrict*
besetzen *to occupy*
besonders *especially*
besprechen (i, a, hat besprochen) *to discuss*
besser *better*
beste *best*
bestehen (a, hat bestanden) *to consist, pass*
bestellen *to order*
bestimmt *certain(ly)*
der **Besuch** *visit*
besuchen *to visit*
das **Bett** *bed*
bevölkern *to populate*
bevor *before*
bezahlen *to pay*
biegen (o, hat gebogen) *to bend, turn*
das **Bier** *beer*
bieten (o, hat geboten) *to offer*
das **Bild** *picture*
billig *cheap*
binden (a, hat gebunden) *to bind, tie*
bis *until, as far as*
das **bißchen** *little bit*
die **Bitte** *request*
bitten (a, hat gebeten) *to request, beg*
bitterlich *bitterly*
blasen (ä, ie, hat geblasen) *to blow*
blaß *pale*
blau *blue*
bleiben (ie, ist geblieben) *to stay, remain*
der **Bleistift** *pencil*
der **Blick** *look, glance*
die **Blume** *flower*
die **Bluse** *blouse*
das **Blut** *blood*
das **Boot** *boat*

böse *bad, angry*
braten (ä, ie, hat gebraten) *to roast, bake, grill, fry*
brauchen *to need*
brechen (i, a, hat/ist gebrochen) *to break*
breit *broad, wide*
die **Breite** *breadth, width*
brennen (brannte, hat gebrannt) *to burn*
das **Brett** *board, plank, shelf, tray*
der **Brief** *letter*
die **Briefmarke** *postage stamp*
die **Brille** *(pair of) spectacles*
bringen (brachte, hat gebracht) *to bring*
das **Brötchen** *bread roll*
die **Brücke** *bridge*
der **Bruder** *brother*
das **Buch** *book*
die **Buche** *beech*
der **Buchstabe** *letter (of the alphabet)*
bunt *brightly coloured, many-coloured*
das **Büro** *office*

das **Café** *café*
das **Camping** *camping*
die **Chance** *luck, chance*
der **Charakter** *character*
der **Chef** *boss*
das **Chlor** *chlorine*
der **Christ** *Christian*
das **Christentum** *Christianity, christendom*
circa *approximately*
Cis *C sharp*
creme *cream (colour)*

da *there, here, then, as*
dabei *near, with it*
das **Dach** *roof*
dadurch *thereby, through it*
dafür *for it*
dagegen *on the other hand, in comparison*

daher *thence, therefore, hence*
dahin *thither, then*
dahinter *behind (it)*
damalig *then (adj.)*
damals *at that time*
damit *in order that, with it*
danach *afterwards, accordingly*
daneben *next to it, in addition*
der **Dank** *thanks*
dankbar *grateful*
die **Dankbarkeit** *gratitude*
dann *then*
daran *thereon, thereat, thereby*
darauf *thereon, then*
daraus *from it*
darin *therein*
darüber *about it, besides*
darum *for that reason, therefore*
darunter *among them, under it*
daß *that*
das **Datum** *date*
davon *about it, therefrom*
der **Deckel** *lid*
dein *your (thy)*
denken (dachte, hat gedacht) *to think*
denn *for, then*
dennoch *yet, nevertheless*
der *the, that one, who, which*
derjenige *the one*
derselbe *the same*
deshalb *for that reason*
desto *the (followed by 'more', 'better' &c)*
deswegen *for that reason*
deutsch *German*
der **Dezember** *December*
dicht *thick, dense, close*
die **Dichte** *density, closeness*
dick *thick, fat*
die **Dicke** *thickness, corpulence*
dienen *to serve*
der **Dienst** *service, post*
dieser, diese, dieses *this, the latter*
das **Ding** *thing*
direkt *direct, straight*
der **Direktor** *director*
diskutieren *to discuss*

doch *but, nevertheless, yes*
das **Dokument** *document*
donnern *to thunder*
der **Donnerstag** *Thursday*
das **Dorf** *village*
dort *there*
dorthin *thither*
das **Drama** *drama, play*
draußen *outside*
das **Drittel** *third (part)*
die **Druckerei** *printing works*
du *you (singular familiar form)*
dumm *stupid*
dunkel *dark*
dünn *thin*
durch *through, by*
durchreisen *to pass through*
dürfen *to be allowed*
der **Durst** *thirst*
das **Dutzend** *dozen*

die **Ebbe** *ebb*
eben *just, very, even*
ebenso *just as*
die **Ecke** *corner*
edel *noble*
die **Ehe** *marriage*
eher *sooner, rather, earlier*
ehren *to honour*
ehrlich *honestly*
das **Ei** *egg*
die **Eiche** *oak*
eigentlich *really*
das **Eigentum** *property*
ein, eine *a, one*
einfach *simple, single*
einige *some, a few*
einladen (ä, u, hat eingeladen) *to invite*
einmal *once*
einmalig *unique*
einschlafen (ä, ie, ist eingeschlafen) *to fall asleep*
die **Einzelheit** *detail*
das **Eisen** *iron*
die **Eisenbahn** *railway*
eisern *(made of) iron*
die **Eleganz** *elegance*

die **Elektrizität** *electricity*
die **Eltern** *parents*
empfangen (ä, i, hat empfangen) *to receive*
empfehlen (ie, a, hat empfohlen) *to recommend*
empfinden (a, hat empfunden) *to feel*
empfindlich *sensitive*
das **Ende** *end*
endgültig *final, definite, conclusive*
endlich *at last*
das **Endspiel** *final round*
der **Engel** *angel*
die **Engländerin** *Englishwoman*
entfalten *to unfold*
entfliehen (o, ist entflohen) *to flee, run away*
entkommen (a, ist entkommen) *to escape*
entnehmen (i, a, hat entnommen) *to take from, infer, gather*
entreißen (i, hat entrissen) *to snatch from*
sich entschließen (o, hat entschlossen) *to decide*
entstehen (a, ist entstanden) *to arise*
enttäuschen *to disappoint*
entweder *either*
entwerfen (i, a, hat entworfen) *to draft, sketch*
entwickeln *to develop*
die **Entwicklung** *development*
entziehen (o, hat entzogen) *to deprive*
das **Erachten** *opinion*
das **Erdbeben** *earthquake*
sich ereignen *to happen*
erfahren (ä, u, hat erfahren) *to experience, learn*
die **Erfahrung** *experience*
erfinden (a, hat erfunden) *to invent, discover*
das **Ergebnis** *result, outcome*
ergreifen (i, hat ergriffen) *to seize*
erhalten (ä, ie, hat erhalten) *to receive*
(sich) erinnern *to remind (remember)*

sich erkälten *to catch cold*
erkennen (erkannte, hat erkannt) *to recognise*
erklären *to explain*
die **Erklärung** *explanation*
erlauben *to permit, allow*
die **Erlaubnis** *permission*
erledigen *to settle, see to*
ermorden *to murder*
ermüdet *tired out*
erreichen *to reach*
der **Ersatz** *replacement*
erscheinen (ie, ist erschienen) *to appear*
erschlagen (ä, u, hat erschlagen) *to slay*
erschließen (o, hat erschlossen) *to open up*
erschrecken (i, a, ist erschrocken) *to be frightened*
erst *first*
erstaunen *to astonish*
erwägen *to weigh*
erwarten *to expect, wait for*
es *it*
essen (i, aß, hat gegessen) *to eat*
die **Etage** *storey*
etwa *about, perhaps*
etwas *something, a bit*
euer *your*
das **Experiment** *experiment*
der **Experte** *expert*

fahren (ä, u, ist gefahren) *to travel, drive*
der **Fahrer** *driver*
die **Fahrkarte** *ticket*
der **Fahrplan** *timetable*
das **Fahrrad** *bicycle*
die **Fahrt** *journey*
der **Fall** *case*
fallen (ä, ie, ist gefallen) *to fall*
falsch *wrong*
die **Familie** *family*
fangen (ä, i, hat gefangen) *to catch*
fast *almost*
faul *lazy*
fechten (i, o, hat gefochten) *to fence*

die **Feder** *pen, feather*
fehlen *to be missing*
der **Fehler** *mistake*
die **Feier** *celebration*
das **Feld** *field*
das **Fenster** *window*
die **Ferien** (pl.) (*school*) *holidays*
fern *far, distant*
die **Ferne** *distance*
fertig *ready, finished*
die **Figur** *figure, form*
der **Film** *film*
finden (**a, hat gefunden**) *to find*
der **Fingerhut** *thimble*
der **Fisch** *fish*
flach *flat*
die **Flasche** *bottle*
flechten (**i, o, hat geflochten**) *to twine, plait*
das **Fleisch** *meat, flesh*
fleißig *industrious*
fliegen (**o, ist geflogen**) *to fly*
fliehen (**o, ist geflohen**) *to flee*
fließen (**o, ist geflossen**) *to flow*
flüchten *to flee, escape*
der **Flüchtling** *refugee*
der **Flug** *flight*
der **Flughafen** *airport*
der **Fluß** *river*
flüstern *to whisper*
folgen *to follow*
die **Forschung** *research*
fort *away, off*
die **Französin** *Frenchwoman*
die **Frau** *woman, lady, Mrs*
das **Fräulein** *young lady, Miss*
frei *free*
das **Freie** *open air*
die **Freiheit** *freedom*
freilich *indeed, of course*
der **Freitag** *Friday*
fremd *strange*
der **Fremde** *stranger*
fressen (**i, a, hat gefressen**) *to eat, feed*
sich **freuen** *to be pleased, look forward*

der **Freund** *friend*
die **Freundin** *female friend, girl friend*
Freundlich *kind*
die **Freundlichkeit** *kindness*
die **Freundschaft** *friendship*
der **Friede** (**n**) *peace*
frieren (**o, hat/ist gefroren**) *to freeze*
froh *glad*
der **Frost** *frost*
die **Frucht** *fruit*
früh *early*
früher *earlier, former(ly)*
der **Frühling** *spring*
das **Frühstück** *breakfast*
der **Fuchs** *fox*
die **Füchsin** *vixen*
fühlen *to feel*
der **Führerschein** *driving licence*
füllen *to fill*
der **Funke** *spark*
für *for*
die **Furcht** *fear*
der **Fuß** *foot*
der **Fußball** *football*

der **Gang** *motion*
ganz *quite, fairly, whole*
die **Garage** *garage*
der **Garten** *garden*
der **Gast** *guest*
das **Gebäck** *confectionery, cakes & pastries*
das **Gebäude** *building*
geben (**i, a, hat gegeben**) *to give*
geboren *born*
die **Geburt** *birth*
das **Gedächtnis** *memory*
der **Gedanke** *thought*
das **Gedicht** *poem*
geduldig *patient*
gefallen (**ä, ie, hat gefallen**) *to please, suit*
das **Gefäß** *vessel, container*
gegen *towards, against, about*
der **Gegensatz** *opposite, opposition*
das **Gegenteil** *opposite, contrary*

gegenüber *opposite, compared with*
das **Gehalt** *salary*
der **Gehalt** *contents*
gehen (i, ist gegangen) *to go, walk*
gehören *to belong*
gehorsam *obedient*
der **Geist** *spirit*
geizig *stingy, miserly*
das **Geld** *money*
der **Gelegenheit** *opportunity*
gelingen (a, ist gelungen) *to succeed*
gelten (i, a, hat gegolten) *to be valid, considered as*
die **Gemeinde** *community, congregation, parish*
gemeinsam *together, joint*
die **Gemeinschaft** *association, community*
das **Gemüse** *vegetable*
genau *exactly, precisely*
der **General** *general*
der **Generaldirektor** *managing director*
das **Genie** *genius*
genießen (o, hat genossen) *to enjoy*
genug *enough, sufficiently*
das **Gepäck** *luggage*
gerade *straight, just*
das **Geräusch** *sound, noise*
das Gericht *law court*
gering *small, slight*
gern *gladly, with pleasure*
der **Geruch** *smell*
der **Gesang** *song, singing*
das **Geschäft** *shop, business*
geschehen (ie, a, ist geschehen) *to happen*
das **Geschenk** *present, gift*
die **Geschichte** *story, history*
das **Geschirr** *crockery*
das **Geschlecht** *sex, gender, race*
der **Geschmack** *taste*
das **Geschrei** *shouting*
die **Geschwindigkeit** *speed*
die **Geschwister** (pl.) *brother(s) and sister(s)*
die **Gesellschaft** *society*

das **Gesetz** *law*
das **Gesicht** *face*
das **Gespräch** *conversation*
gestern *yesterday*
gesund *healthy*
die **Gesundheit** *health*
das **Gewicht** *weight*
gewinnen (a, hat gewonnen) *to win*
gewiß *certain(ly)*
das **Gewitter** *storm, thunderstorm*
gewöhnen *to accustom*
die **Gewohnheit** *habit, custom*
gewöhnlich *usually, normally*
gießen (o, hat gegossen) *to pour*
das **Glas** *glass*
der **Glaube(n)** *belief*
glauben *to believe*
gleich *same, immediately*
gleiten (i, ist geglitten) *to slide, glide*
das **Glück** *luck, good fortune*
glücklich *happy, lucky*
glücklicherweise *fortunately*
das **Gold** *gold*
golden *gold, golden*
graben (ä, u, hat gegraben) *to dig*
der **Grad** *degree*
gratulieren *to congratulate*
greifen (i, hat gegriffen) *to seize, grasp, catch*
grob *coarse*
groß *large, tall, great*
die **Größe** *size*
großzügig *generous*
grün *green*
der **Grund** *ground, cause*
die **Grundlage** *basis*
gründlich *thorough(ly)*
der **Grundsatz** *principle*
die **Grundschule** *primary school*
die **Grundzahl** *cardinal number*
gucken *to look, peep*
gut *good*

das **Haar** *hair*
haben (hatte, hat gehabt) *to have*
hageln *to hail*
halb *half*

die **Hälfte** *half*
halten (ä, ie, hat gehalten) *to hold, stop*
die **Hand** *hand*
handeln *to deal, trade*
der **Handschuh** *glove*
hängen (i, hat gehangen) *to hang*
hart *hard*
hassen *to hate*
der **Haufen** *pile, heap*
der **Hauptbahnhof** *main station*
der **Hauptmann** *Captain*
die **Hauptsache** *most important thing*
die **Hauptstadt** *capital city*
das **Haus** *house*
das **Häuschen** *little house, cottage*
heben (o, hat gehoben) *to raise, lift*
das **Heft** *exercise book*
heilen *to heal*
heißen (ie, hat geheißen) *to be called*
der **Held** *hero*
helfen (i, a, hat geholfen) *to help*
das **Hemd** *shirt*
her *hither, here, this way*
herauf *up, from below*
heraus *out*
der **Herbst** *autumn*
der **Herr** *gentleman, Mr, Lord, master*
herum *around*
hervor *forth*
das **Herz** *heart*
das **Heu** *hay*
heute *today*
heutig *of today, present day*
hier *here*
hierher *hither*
der **Himmel** *sky, heaven(s)*
hin *thither*
hinauf *up*
das **Hindernis** *hindrance, obstacle*
hindurch *through*
hinein *in, inside*
hinter *behind*
der **Hinweis** *hint, indication*
hinweisen (ie, hat hingewiesen) *to show, point to, point out*

historisch *historic(al)*
hoch *high*
hoffen *to hope*
die **Hoffnung** *hope*
die **Höhe** *height*
hören *to hear*
das **Hotel** *hotel*
hübsch *pretty*
der **Hund** *dog*
die **Hündin** *bitch*
der **Hunger** *hunger*
der **Hut** *hat*

ich *I*
ihr *you, her*
die **Illusion** *illusion*
immer *always, ever*
immerhin *still, nevertheless*
in *in, at, into*
indem *while*
indessen *meanwhile, however*
die **Industrie** *industry*
die **Infektion** *infection*
informieren *to inform*
der **Ingenieur** *engineer*
innere *inner, interior*
innerhalb *inside*
die **Insel** *island*
die **Intelligenz** *intelligence*
interessant *interesting*
interessieren *to interest*
inzwischen *meanwhile*
irgend *any, some*
(sich) irren *to be mistaken*
der **Irrtum** *error, mistake*

ja *yes, of course, you know*
das **Jahr** *year*
die **Jalousie** *venetian blind*
der **Januar** *January*
je *ever, apiece, the*
jeder, jede, jedes *every*
jedoch *however*
jemand *someone*
jener, jene, jenes *that, yon, the former*
jetzt *now*

das **Jod** *iodine*
das **Journal** *magazine, newspaper*
die **Jugend** *youth*
der **Juli** *July*
jung *young*
der **Junge** *boy*
der **Juni** *June*

der **Kaffee** *coffee*
der **Käfig** *cage*
kahl *bare, bald*
kalt *cold*
die **Kälte** *cold, coldness*
der **Kamerad** *comrade, companion*
kämpfen *to fight, strive*
die **Karte** *card, menu, map*
der **Käse** *cheese*
die **Katze** *cat*
kaufen *to buy*
kaum *scarcely*
kehren *to turn, sweep*
kein *not one, not a*
kennen (kannte, hat gekannt) *to know (persons, places)*
die **Kenntnis** *knowledge*
der **Kiefer** *jaw*
die **Kiefer** *pine*
das **Kilo(gramm)** *kilogram*
das/der **Kilometer** *kilometre*
das **Kind** *child*
kindlich *childlike*
die **Kirche** *church*
die **Kirsche** *cherry*
klagen *to complain*
klar *clear(ly)*
die **Klasse** *class*
das **Kleid** *dress*
klein *small*
klettern *to climb, scramble*
klingeln *to ring (of a bell)*
klingen (a, hat geklungen) *to sound, ring*
klopfen *to knock, tap*
das **Kloster** *monastery, convent*
klug *intelligent, clever*
knapp *barely*
der **Knopf** *button*

kochen *to boil, cook*
der **Kollege** *colleague*
komisch *funny, odd*
das **Komma** *comma*
kommen (a, ist gekommen) *to come*
der **Kommunismus** *communism*
der **Komponist** *composer*
der **Konferenz** *conference*
der **König** *king*
die **Königin** *queen*
das **Königreich** *kingdom*
können *to be able to*
kontrollieren *to check*
das **Konzert** *concert, concerto*
der **Kopf** *head*
der **Korkenzieher** *corkscrew*
kosten *to cost*
der **Kran** *crane*
krank *ill*
kriechen (o, ist gekrochen) *to creep, crawl*
der **Krieg** *war*
die **Krise** *crisis*
die **Kritik** *criticism*
der **Kuchen** *cake*
die **Kuh** *cow*
der **Kunde** *customer*
das **Kupfer** *copper*
kurz *short*
kürzlich *recently*
kurzsichtig *short-sighted*

das **Laboratorium** *laboratory*
lächeln *to smile*
lachen *to laugh*
laden (ä, u, hat geladen) *to load*
der **Laden** *shop*
die **Lage** *situation*
die **Lampe** *lamp*
das **Land** *land, country*
lang *long*
die **Länge** *length*
langsam *slowly*
längst *long ago, long since*
langweilig *boring*
die **Lärche** *larch*
lassen (ä, ie, hat gelassen) *to leave*

laufen (äu, ie, ist gelaufen) *to run*
die **Laune** *mood, temper*
laut *loud(ly)*
der **Laut** *sound*
leben *to live*
das **Leben** *life*
die **Lebensmittel** (pl.) *foodstuffs*
lediglich *solely*
leer *empty*
legen *to lay*
lehren *to teach*
der **Lehrer** *teacher*
die **Lehrerin** *woman teacher*
der **Lehrling** *apprentice*
leicht *light, easy*
leiden (i, hat gelitten) *to suffer*
leider *unfortunately, more's the pity*
leihen (ie, hat geliehen) *to lend*
(sich) leisten *to achieve (afford)*
der **Leiter** *leader, chief, conductor*
die **Leiter** *ladder*
lesen (ie, a, hat gelesen) *to read*
letzte *last*
leuchten *to shine*
die **Leute** (pl.) *people*
das **Licht** *light*
lieb *dear, beloved*
lieber *rather*
das **Lied** *song*
liegen (a, hat gelegen) *to lie*
lila *lilac (colour)*
links *left, on the left-hand side*
das **Liter** *litre*
loben *to praise*
das **Loch** *hole*
der **Löffel** *spoon*
los *loose, off*!
losbrechen (i, a, ist losgebrochen) *to break loose*
lösen *to loosen, solve*
losfahren (ä, u, ist losgefahren) *to drive off, set off*
die **Lösung** *solution*
der **Löwe** *lion*
die **Löwin** *lioness*
die **Luft** *air*
lügen (o, hat gelogen) *to tell lies*

machen *to make, to do*
die **Macht** *might, power*
mächtig *powerful*
machtlos *powerless*
das **Mädchen** *girl*
der **Mai** *May*
mal (abbr. of **einmal**) *times, just*
das **Mal** *(point of) time*
der **Maler** *painter*
man *one*
manch *many (a)*
der **Mann** *man*
der **Männlein** *little man*
die **Mannschaft** *team*
der **Mantel** *coat*
das **Märchen** *(fairy) tale*
die **Mark** *mark (unit of German currency)*
der **Marktplatz** *market place*
der **März** *March*
der **Matrose** *sailor*
matt *weak, dull*
die **Maus** *mouse*
das **Mehl** *flour*
mehr *more*
mehrere *several*
mein *my, mine*
meinen *to think, mean*
meinetwegen *so far as I am concerned*
die **Meinung** *opinion*
meistens *usually, for the most part*
die **Melodie** *melody, tune*
der **Mensch** *human being, person*
merkwürdig *remarkable, curious*
merkwürdigerweise *strange to say*
messen (i, a, hat gemessen) *to measure*
der **Messer** *surveyor, gauge*
das **Messer** *knife*
das **Metall** *metal*
das/der **Meter** *metre*
die **Milch** *milk*
der **Militärdienst** *military service*
die **Million** *million*
der **Millionär** *millionaire*
mindestens *at least*
der **Ministerpräsident** *prime minister*

die **Minute** *minute*
mißachten *to despise, undervalue*
der **Mißbrauch** *misuse*
der **Mißerfolg** *failure*
mißglücken *to fail, miscarry*
mißhandeln *to ill-treat*
die **Mißhandlung** *ill-treatment*
mißlingen *to fail*
das **Mißverständnis** *misunderstanding*
mißverstehen *to misunderstand*
mit *with, by*
der **Mitarbeiter** *colleague, workmate*
das **Mitglied** *member*
das **Mitleid** *sympathy*
mitnehmen *to take with one*
der **Mitreisende** *fellow traveller*
der **Mittag** *midday*
das **Mittagessen** *midday meal, lunch*
die **Mitte** *middle*
mitteilen *to inform*
der **Mittwoch** *Wednesday*
die **Mode** *fashion, custom*
das **Modell** *model*
modern *modern*
mögen *to like, wish*
möglich *possible*
der **Moment** *moment*
das **Moment** *momentum, factor*
der **Monat** *month*
der **Montag** *Monday*
der **Mord** *murder*
morgen *tomorrow*
der **Morgen** *morning*
morgens *in the morning(s)*
der **Motor** *engine*
müde *tired*
das **Münster** *minster*
die **Musik** *music*
müssen *to have to, be obliged to*
die **Mutter** *mother*

na! *well!*
nach *after, to*
nachdem *after*
nachdenken *to reflect, ponder*
nachher *later, afterwards*

nachmittags *in the afternoon*
die **Nachricht** *news*
nächste *next, nearest, closest*
die **Nacht** *night*
nachts *at night*
nah *near*
der **Name** *name*
nämlich *namely, because, you see*
naß *wet*
die **Nation** *nation*
die **Natur** *nature*
der **Nebel** *mist, fog*
neben *next to, near*
der **Neffe** *nephew*
nehmen (i, a, hat genommen) *to take*
nein *no*
die **Nelke** *carnation, pink*
nennen (nannte, hat genannt) *to name*
der **Nerv** *nerve*
neu *new*
nicht *not*
nichts *nothing*
nicken *to nod*
nie *never*
nieder *down*
niemand *nobody, no one*
noch *still, yet, besides*
normalerweise *normally*
der **November** *November*
die **Null** *zero, nought*
nun *now, well*
nur *only*

ob *whether*
oben *upstairs, above, on top*
ober *upper*
oberhalb *above*
obgleich *although*
das **Obst** *fruit*
obwohl *although*
der **Ochs** *ox*
oder *or*
der **Ofen** *oven, stove*
offen *open*
öffnen *to open*
oft *often*

ohne *without*
das **Ohr** *ear*
oliv *olive (coloured)*
die **Oma** *grandma*
der **Onkel** *uncle*
die **Oper** *opera*
orange *orange (coloured)*
ordnen *to arrange, sort, regulate*
die **Ordnung** *order, tidiness*
das **Organ** *organ*
organisieren *to organise*
orientieren *to orientate*
der **Osten** *east*
das **Ostern** *Easter*
der **Ozean** *ocean*

paar *few*
das **Paar** *pair*
packen *to seize, grab, pack*
der **Palast** *palace*
der **Park** *park*
die **Partei** *political party*
passen *to suit*
passieren *to happen*
der **Patient** *patient (medical)*
die **Patientin** *female patient*
der **Pfad** *path*
die **Pfahl** *pole*
die **Pfanne** *pan*
der **Pfeffer** *pepper*
die **Pfeife** *pipe*
pfeifen (i, hat gepfiffen) *to whistle*
der **Pfennig** *penny, pfennig (hundredth of a mark)*
pflanzen *to plant*
pflücken *to pluck, pick*
das **Pfund** *pound*
die **Phantasie** *imagination*
der **Phosphor** *phosphorus*
die **Physik** *physics*
der **Plan** *plan, map*
planmäßig *scheduled, according to plan*
der **Plast** *plastic*
der **Platz** *square, seat, room, place*
platzen *to burst*
plaudern *to chat*

plötzlich *sudden(ly)*
die **Polizei** *police*
der **Polizist** *policeman*
die **Post** *post (office)*
praktisch *practical(ly)*
der **Präsident** *president*
das **Präteritum** *preterite, simple past tense*
der **Preis** *price, prize*
probieren *to sample*
das **Problem** *problem*
produzieren *to produce*
der **Professor** *professor*
die **Prosa** *prose*
das **Prozent** *per cent*
putzen *to clean, polish*

das **Quadrat** *square*
die **Qualität** *quality*

das **Radio** *radio*
der **Rand** *edge*
rasch *quick(ly)*
(sich) rasieren *to shave*
raten (ä, ie, hat geraten) *to advise*
das **Rätsel** *puzzle*
rauchen *to smoke*
rechnen *to calculate*
recht *right, quite*
rechts *right-hand side*
reden *to talk*
die **Regel** *rule*
der **Regen** *rain*
regieren *to rule, govern*
die **Regierung** *government*
regnen *to rain*
reiben (ie, hat gerieben) *to rub, grate*
reich *rich*
der **Reichtum** *riches, wealth*
die **Reihe** *row, sequence, turn*
rein *pure, clean*
reisen *to travel*
reißen (i, hat/ist gerissen) *to tear*
reiten (i, ist geritten) *to ride*
rennen (rannte, ist gerannt) *to run*
reparieren *to repair*
die **Republik** *republic*

reservieren *to reserve, book*
das **Restaurant** *restaurant*
retten *to save*
die **Revolution** *revolution*
richtig *right, correct*
riechen (**o, hat gerochen**) *to smell*
der **Ring** *ring*
rings *around*
der **Rock** *skirt*
roh *raw*
der **Roman** *novel*
rosa *rose (coloured), pink*
die **Rose** *rose*
rot *red*
der **Rückblick** *glance, back*
die **Rückfahrt** *return journey*
die **Rückkehr** *return*
der **Rücksitz** *back seat*
rückwärts *backwards*
rudern *to row*
rufen (**ie, hat gerufen**) *to call, shout*
ruhig *peaceful, quiet(ly)*
rund *round, about*
russisch *Russian*

die **Sache** *thing*
der **Sack** *sack*
sagen *to say*
der **Salat** *salad*
der **Same** *seed*
die **Sammlung** *collection*
der **Samstag** *Saturday*
satt *full, satiated, sick*
der **Satz** *sentence*
die **Sau** *sow*
der **Schaden** *damage*
schädlich *detrimental*
schaffen (**u, hat geschaffen**) *to create*
scharf *sharp, strong*
der **Schauspieler** *actor*
der **Scheck** *cheque*
der **Schein** *banknote, form, appearance*
scheinen (**ie, hat geschienen**) *to shine, seem*
schelten (**i, a, hat gescholten**) *to scold*

schenken *to give, present*
schicken *to send*
schieben (**o, hat geschoben**) *to push, shove*
schießen (**o, hat geschossen**) *to shoot*
das **Schiff** *ship*
der **Schild** *shield*
das **Schild** *sign-board, plate*
der **Schilling** *shilling (unit of Austrian currency)*
der **Schlaf** *sleep*
schlafen (**ä, ie, hat geschlafen**) *to sleep*
schlagen (**ä, u, hat geschlagen**) *to hit*
schlank *slim, slender*
schlecht *bad*
schließen (**o, hat geschlossen**) *to close, shut*
schlimm *bad, unpleasant*
der **Schlüssel** *key*
schmecken *to taste*
schmelzen (**i, o, hat/ist geschmolzen**) *to melt, smelt*
der **Schmerz** *pain*
der **Schmuck** *jewellery, ornament*
schmutzig *dirty*
der **Schnaps** *Schnapps, spirits*
der **Schnee** *snow*
schneiden (**i, hat geschnitten**) *to cut*
schneien *to snow*
schnell *fast, quick(ly)*
schon *already*
schön *beautiful*
schreiben (**ie, hat geschrieben**) *to write*
die **Schreibmaschine** *typewriter*
der **Schreibtisch** *desk*
schreien (**ie, hat geschrieen**) *to cry out, scream*
schreiten (**i, ist geschritten**) *to stride*
schrittweise *step by step*
der **Schuh** *shoe*
schuldig *owing, guilty*
die **Schule** *school*
der **Schüler** *schoolboy*
die **Schülerin** *schoolgirl*
die **Schüssel** *dish, bowl*

schützen *to protect*
schwach *weak*
schwarz *black*
der **Schwefel** *sulphur*
schweigen (ie, hat geschwiegen) *to be silent*
schwer *heavy, difficult*
die **Schwere** *weight*
schwerlich *hardly*
die **Schwester** *sister*
schwierig *difficult*
die **Schwierigkeit** *difficulty*
schwimmen (a, ist geschwommen) *to swim*
schwören (o, hat geschworen) *to swear, take an oath*
der **See** *lake*
die **See** *sea*
sehen (ie, a, hat gesehen) *to see*
sehr *very*
sein (ist, war, ist gewesen) *to be*
sein, seine *his, its*
seit *since (preposition)*
seitdem *since (conjunction)*
selber, selbst *self, personally*
senden (sandte, gesandt) *to send*
(sich) setzen *to put (sit down)*
sich *him/her/it/yourself, your/themselves, each other*
sie *she, they, it*
Sie *you*
das **Silber** *silver*
singen (a, hat gesungen) *to sing*
sinken (a, ist gesunken) *to sink*
der **Sinn** *sense, mind, meaning*
die **Sitte** *custom*
sitzen (a, hat gesessen) *to be seated, sit*
die **Sitzung** *sitting, meeting*
so *so, thus*
das **Sofa** *sofa*
sofort *immediately, quickly*
sogar *even*
sogleich *right away, immediately*
der **Sohn** *son*
solcher, solche, solches *such (a)*
der **Soldat** *soldier*

sollen *to be supposed to (ought)*
der **Sommer** *summer*
sondern *but*
die **Sonne** *sun*
der **Sonntag** *Sunday*
sonst *otherwise*
sorgfältig *careful(ly)*
der **Sozialismus** *socialism*
sparen *to save*
der **Spaß** *fun*
spät *late*
der **Spaten** *spade*
spazieren *to stroll, take a walk*
der **Spaziergang** *walk*
das **Spiel** *game*
spielen *to play*
die **Spitzengeschwindigkeit** *top speed*
die **Spitzenleistung** *peak output*
das **Spitzenwert** *peak value*
die **Spitzenzeiten** (pl.) *peak period, rush hours*
das **Sprachgefühl** *feeling for language*
sprechen (i, a, hat gesprochen) *to speak*
springen (a, ist gesprungen) *to jump*
der **Staat** *state*
das **Stadion** *stadium*
die **Stadt** *town*
der **Staffellauf** *relay race*
stammen *to originate from*
stark *strong*
statt *instead of*
stattfinden (fand statt, hat stattgefunden) *to take place*
stechen (i, a, hat gestochen) *to sting*
stehen (a, hat gestanden) *to stand*
stehlen (ie, a, hat gestohlen) *to steal*
steigen (ie, ist gestiegen) *to climb*
steinreich *immensely rich*
die **Stelle** *place, position*
sterben (i, a, ist gestorben) *to die*
stets *always*
das **Steuer** *steering wheel*
die **Steuer** *tax*
der **Stich** *stab, sting*

der **Stift** *nail, pencil*
das **Stift** *institution, home*
die **Stimme** *voice, vote*
stimmen *to be correct*
der **Stock** *stick, storey*
stöhnen *to groan*
stolz *proud*
stören *to disturb*
stoßen (ö, ie, ist/hat gestossen) *to knock*
der **Strahl** *beam*
die **Straße** *street*
der **Strauß** *bunch of flowers, ostrich*
der **Streik** *strike (industrial)*
streiten (i, hat gestritten) *to quarrel*
der **Strich** *stroke, line*
stricken *to knit*
der **Strom** *current, river*
das **Stück** *piece, bit*
der **Student** *student*
die **Studentin** *female student*
der **Studienrat** *secondary school teacher*
studieren *to study*
das **Studium** *study*
die **Stunde** *hour, lesson*
stürzen *to plunge, rush*
suchen *to seek*
der **Süden** *south*
südlich *south*
die **Suppe** *soup*
süß *sweet*

tadeln *to blame, tell off*
der **Tag** *day*
taktlos *tactless*
das **Talent** *talent*
die **Tante** *aunt*
tanzen *to dance*
die **Tasse** *cup*
die **Tat** *deed*
die **Tatsache** *fact*
taugen *to be worth, fit for*
technisch *technical(ly)*
der **Tee** *tea*
der **Teich** *pond, pool*
der **Teil** *part*

das **Teil** *share*
teilnehmen (i, a, hat teilgenommen) *to take part*
teilweise *partly*
das **Telefon** *telephone*
telefonieren *to telephone*
die **Temperatur** *temperature*
teuer *dear, expensive*
das **Theater** *theatre*
das **Thema** *theme, subject*
der **Tisch** *table*
der **Tischler** *joiner, carpenter*
die **Tochter** *daughter*
der **Tod** *death*
die **Toleranz** *tolerance*
die **Tonne** *ton, tonne (1,000 kg)*
der **Tor** *fool*
das **Tor** *gate, goal (in sport)*
die **Torte** *cake, tart, flan*
tragen (ä, u, hat getragen) *to carry, wear*
trainieren *to train*
trauern *to mourn*
träumen *to dream*
traurig *sad*
treffen (i, a, hat getroffen) *to meet, befall*
treiben (ie, hat getrieben) *to drive, practise*
die **Treppe** *stairs*
treten (i, a, hat/ist getreten) *to step*
treu *faithful*
treulich *faithfully*
trinken (a, hat getrunken) *to drink*
trocknen *to dry*
der **Tropfen** *drop*
trotz *in spite of, despite*
trotzdem *nevertheless*
das **Tuch** *cloth*
die **Tulpe** *tulip*
tun (tat, hat getan) *to do*
die **Tür** *door*

übel *bad, unpleasant, ill*
über *over, above, about*
überall *everywhere*

das **Überbleibsel** *remnant, leftover*
der **Übergang** *crossing*
die **Überraschung** *surprise*
übersetzen *to translate, ferry*
übertreten *to violate, overflow*
überzeugen *to convince*
übrig *left over, to spare*
übrigens *anyway, besides*
die **Uhr** *time, clock, watch, o'clock*
um *around, about, at*
der **Umstand** *circumstance*
(sich) umziehen *to change clothes, move house, become overcast*
die **Unabhängigkeit** *independence*
unaufhörlich *ceaselessly*
und *and*
unerhört *scandalous, unheard of*
ungefähr *roughly, about, approximately*
unglaublich *incredible*
das **Unglück** *misfortune*
die **Universität** *university*
unmittelbar *immediate(ly), direct(ly)*
die **Unordnung** *disorder*
unrecht *wrong*
die **Unruhe** *unrest*
unser, unsere *our*
unten *downstairs, beneath, below*
unter *under, among*
untergehen (i, ist untergegangen) *to sink, set*
unterhalb *below*
(sich) unterhalten (ä, ie, hat unterhalten) *to converse, maintain, entertain*
der **Unterschied** *difference, distinction*
unvergeßlich *unforgettable*
unwahrscheinlich *improbable*
die **Uraufführung** *first performance*
die **Urgroßmutter** *great grandmother*
die **Urkunde** *title deed, document*
der **Urlaub** *holiday, leave*
die **Ursache** *cause*
der **Ursprung** *origin*
urteilen *to judge*

die **Vase** *vase*
der **Vater** *father*
sich verabschieden *to take one's leave*
verändern *to change, alter*
veranstalten *to organise*
verbessern *to improve, correct*
verbringen (verbrachte, hat verbracht) *to spend (time)*
verbunden *obliged, indebted*
verderben (i, a, hat verdorben) *to spoil, ruin*
der **Verdienst** *earnings*
das **Verdienst** *merit*
vereinfachen *to simplify*
das **Verfahren** *process*
verfügen *to dispose*
die **Verfügung** *disposal*
vergehen (i, ist vergangen) *to pass*
vergessen (i, a, hat vergessen) *to forget*
vergrößert *magnified*
das **Verhältnis** *relationship*
verheiratet *married*
verkaufen *to sell*
der **Verkäufer** *salesman*
der **Verkehrsunfall** *traffic accident*
verkennen *to misjudge*
(sich) verlassen (ä, ie, hat verlassen) *to leave (rely)*
verlernen *to unlearn, forget*
verletzen *to injure, wound*
verliebt *in love*
verlieren (o, hat verloren) *to lose*
vermeiden (ie, hat vermieden) *to avoid*
verpassen *to miss (a train, an opportunity)*
verplaudern *to chatter time away*
verraten (ä, ie, hat verraten) *to betray*
verreisen *to go on a journey*
verschieben (o, hat verschoben) *to postpone*
verschließen (o, hat verschlossen) *to close, shut*
verschwinden (a, hat verschwunden) *to disappear*

versprechen (i, a, hat versprochen) *to promise*

verstehen (a, hat verstanden) *to understand*

versuchen *to attempt, try, tempt*

vertauschen *to exchange*

verteidigen *to defend*

der **Vertrag** *contract, treaty, pact*

vertreiben (ie, hat vertrieben) *to drive away, banish*

verwandt *related*

der/die **Verwandte** *relation*

verwechseln *to confuse, mix up, mistake*

verzeihen (ie, hat verziehen) *to pardon, excuse*

verzichten *to forgo, do without*

der **Vetter** *(male) cousin*

viel *much, many, a lot*

vielfach *manifold, multifarious*

das **Viertel** *quarter, district*

der **Vogel** *bird*

voll *full*

von *from, by*

vor *in front of, before*

voraussagen *to predict*

voraussetzen *to presuppose, assume*

die **Voraussetzung** *requirement, precondition*

vorenthalten (ä, ie, hat vorenthalten) *to withhold*

vorher *before, earlier*

vorkommen (a, ist vorgekommen) *to occur*

vorläufig *provisional(ly)*

vorn(e) *in (the) front*

der **Vorschlag** *suggestion, proposal*

die **Vorschrift** *regulation, rule*

(sich) **vorstellen** *to introduce (oneself; to imagine)*

vorwärts *forward*

vorziehen (o, hat vorgezogen) *to prefer*

wachsen (ä, u, ist gewachsen) *to grow*

die **Waffe** *weapon*

wagen *to venture, dare*

der **Wagen** *motor car*

wählen *to choose, elect*

wahr *true*

während *during*

die **Wahrheit** *truth*

der **Wald** *wood, forest*

die **Wand** *(interior) wall*

wann *when*

warm *warm, hot*

warnen *to warn*

warten *to wait*

warum *why*

was *what, that*

waschen (ä, u, hat gewaschen) *to wash*

das **Wasser** *water*

weder ... noch *neither ... nor*

weg *away*

der **Weg** *way, path*

wegen *on account of, because of*

weggehen (i, ist weggegangen) *to go away*

wegnehmen *to take away*

das **Weib** *woman*

weich *soft*

das **Weihnachten** (also pl.) *Christmas*

weil *because*

der **Wein** *wine*

weinen *to cry, weep*

die **Weise** *manner, way*

weisen (ie, hat gewiesen) *to point out*

weiß *white*

weit *wide, large, far, distant*

weiter *further*

weitergehen (i, ist weitergegangen) *to go on*

welcher, welche, welches *which, what*

wenden (wandte, hat gewandt) *to turn*

wenig *little, few*

wenigstens *at least*

wenn *if, whenever, although*

wer *who*

werden (i, u, ist geworden) *to become*

werfen (i, a, hat geworfen)

das **Werk** *work, factory*

wert *worth, worthy*

wertvoll *valuable*
weshalb *wherefore*
das **Wetter** *weather*
wichtig *important*
wider *against, contrary to*
wie *how*
wieder *again*
**wiedersehen (ie, a, hat wiederge-
  sehen)** *to see again*
wiegen (o, hat gewogen) *to weigh*
wieso *how so, why*
der **Wille(n)** *will, purpose*
willkommen *welcome*
der **Wind** *wind*
der **Winter** *winter*
wirklich *really*
wissen (weiß, wußte, hat gewußt) *to
  know*
wo *where*
die **Woche** *week*
woher *whence*
wohin *whither*
wohl *well, healthy, probably*
die **Wohlfahrt** *welfare*
das **Wohlsein** *wellbeing*
der **Wohlstand** *prosperity*
das **Wohlwollen** *goodwill*
wohnen *to live, dwell*
die **Wohnung** *apartment, flat*
die **Wolke** *cloud*
wollen *to want, wish*
womit *with what, wherewith*
woran *whereon, whereat*
worauf *whereupon, at what*
das **Wort** *word*
wovon *whereof, concerning which*
wozu *for what purpose, why*
die **Wunde** *wound*
wünschen *to wish*
die **Wurst** *sausage*

die **Zahl** *number*

zahlen *to pay*
zählen *to count*
zahm *tame*
der **Zahn** *tooth*
zart *gentle, delicate*
die **Zeit** *time*
die **Zeitung** *newspaper*
der **Zentner** *hundredweight (50 kg in
  West and East Germany, 100 kg in
  Austria & Switzerland)*
zerbrechen (i, a, hat zerbrochen) *to
  smash, shatter*
zerreißen (i, hat zerrissen) *to tear
  (up)*
zerstören *to destroy*
das **Zeugnis** *evidence, certificate*
ziehen (o, hat/ist gezogen) *to pull,
  move*
ziemlich *fairly, quite, rather*
die **Zigarette** *cigarette*
das **Zitat** *quotation*
zitieren *to quote*
zittern *to tremble*
der **Zoll** *customs, inch*
zu *to, at*
zufrieden *content, pleased*
der **Zug** *train*
zuhören *to listen*
die **Zunge** *tongue*
zurück *back*
zurückkehren *to return, go back*
zusammen *together*
zwar *indeed, certainly*
der **Zweifel** *doubt*
zweifeln *to doubt*
der **Zweig** *twig*
das **Zwiegespräch** *dialogue*
der **Zwilling** *twin*
zwingen (a, hat gezwungen) *to force,
  compel*
zwischen *between*